DOWN TO EARTH

*Cycle C Sermons Based on the Second Lessons for Advent,
Christmas, and Epiphany*

Scott Bryte & Kimberly Miller van Driel

CSS Publishing Company, Inc.
Lima, Ohio

DOWN TO EARTH

FIRST EDITION
Copyright © 2021
by CSS Publishing Co., Inc.

The original purchaser may print and photocopy material in this publication for use as it was intended (worship material for worship use; educational material for classroom use; dramatic material for staging or production). No additional permission is required from the publisher for such copying by the original purchaser only. Inquiries should be addressed to: Permissions, CSS Publishing Company, Inc., 5450 N. Dixie Highway, Lima, Ohio 45807.

[Scripture quotations are] from the New Revised Standard Version of the Bible, copyright © 1989 by the National Council of the Churches of Christ in the USA. Used by permission. All rights reserved

Library of Congress Cataloging-in-Publication Data

Names: Bryte, Scott, 1963- author. | Miller van Driel, Kimberly, 1978- author. Title: Down to earth : Cycle C sermons based on second lessons for Advent, Christmas, and Epiphany / Scott Bryte & Kimberly Miller van Driel. Description: First edition. | Lima, Ohio : CSS Publishing Company, Inc., [2021] Identifiers: LCCN 2021017615 | ISBN 9780788030208 (paperback) | ISBN 0788030213 | ISBN 9780788030215 (ebook) | ISBN 0788030205 (digitall printed) Subjects: LCSH: Bible. New Testament--Sermons. | Common lectionary (1992). Year C. | Advent sermons. | Christmas sermons. | Epiphany--Sermons. Classification: LCC BS2341.55 .B79 2021 | DDC 252/.61--dc23 LC record available at https://lccn.loc.gov/2021017615

For more information about CSS Publishing Company resources, visit our website at www.csspub.com, email us at csr@csspub.com, or call (800) 241-4056.

e-book:
ISBN-13: 978-0-7880-3021-5
ISBN-10: 0-7880-3021-3

ISBN-13: 978-0-7880-3020-8
ISBN-10: 0-7880-3020-5   DIGITALLY PRINTED

CONTENTS

Comma — 5
First Sunday of Advent (SB)
1 Thessalonians 3:9-13

Life In The Future — 8
Second Sunday of Advent (SB)
Philippians 1:3-11

Don't Worry, Be Peaceful — 12
Third Sunday of Advent (SB)
Philippians 4:4-7

Not A Religion — 16
Fourth Sunday of Advent (SB)
Hebrews 10:5-10

But, Why? — 19
Nativity of Our Lord (SB)
Titus 3:4-7

Put On Christ — 22
First Sunday after Christmas Day (SB)
Colossians 3:12-17

What's New? — 26
New Year's Day (SB)
Revelation 21:1-6a

The Good Kind Of Awkward — 30
Second Sunday after Christmas Day (SB)
Ephesians 1:3-14

"Aha" Moment — 34
Epiphany of Our Lord (SB)
Ephesians 3:1-12

But, What Does It Do?   *39*
Baptism of Our Lord/First Sunday after the Epiphany (SB)
Acts 8:14-17

Gifted   *43*
Second Sunday after the Epiphany (SB)
1 Corinthians 12:1-11

Parts Is Parts   *47*
Third Sunday after the Epiphany (SB)
1 Corinthians 12:12-31a

Who's Love?   *51*
Fourth Sunday after the Epiphany (KvD)
1 Corinthians 13:1-13

Does Millard Fillmore Really Matter?   *55*
Fifth Sunday after the Epiphany (SB)
1 Corinthians 15:1-11

Elevator Speech   *59*
Sixth Sunday after the Epiphany (SB)
1 Corinthians 15:12-20

Juke A Box   *63*
Seventh Sunday after the Epiphany (KvD)
1 Corinthians 15:35-38; 42-50

Behind The Veil   *67*
Transfiguration Sunday (SB)
2 Corinthians 3:12—4:2

The More Things Change...   *71*
Eighth Sunday after the Epiphany (SB)
1 Corinthians 15:51-58

Just One   *75*
Ninth Sunday after the Epiphany (KvD)
Galatians 1:1-12

First Sunday of Advent (SB)

1 Thessalonians 3:9-13

Comma

How can we thank God enough for you in return for all the joy that we feel before our God because of you? Night and day, we pray most earnestly that we may see you face to face and restore whatever is lacking in your faith.

Now may our God and Father himself and our Lord Jesus direct our way to you. And may the Lord make you increase and abound in love for one another and for all, just as we abound in love for you. And may he so strengthen your hearts in holiness that you may be blameless before our God and Father at the coming of our Lord Jesus with all his saints.

The Season of Advent begins today. It's a new season in the church and there's a new look. The Advent wreath is out. There's blue or violet stuff on the altar and elsewhere. Out in the world around us, and maybe in our homes as well, things are beginning to look a lot like Christmas. You might have an Advent wreath with four candles around somewhere. Maybe you have an Advent calendar to help you with the countdown. Advent calendars are actually a Lutheran invention; they have been in use since the nineteenth century. Advent calendars have flaps that are opened one by one during the days of December leading up to Christmas. There are 24 flaps for 24 days of Advent, plus one more for Christmas day itself. Sometimes there are pictures behind the doors. Other times there are Bible verses. Occasionally there are little compartments to hide tiny gifts. Advent calendars are a fun tradition that gets it mostly right — kind of.

The season of Advent begins four Sundays before Christmas. Advent always ends on December 24, but its starting date changes.

Down To Earth

Its first day is not always on December 1 but can fall anywhere from November 27 to December 3. Sometimes, Advent is 24 days long like the Advent calendars allow, but not always. There can be as few as 22 days in Advent, or as many as 28, depending on the day of the week on which Christmas Day falls. Advent calendars get the number of days right one year out of every seven.

No matter when it begins, or how many days it lasts, the season of Advent looks toward the celebration of Christmas. It looks to the incarnation, when our holy and far off God, the one separate from the grubby reality that we live in; above the pettiness and the meanness, the cruelty and the thoughtlessness that holds us down, and beyond our limited understanding, became one of us. In the incarnation, God was united with us, not in a spiritual way, not just as a metaphor, but in the physical sense. God became one of us. In Jesus, God shared our DNA. In Jesus, God lived the kind of life that we live — ups and downs, aches and pains, all the excitement and the annoyances too. In Jesus, God is united with us. That incarnation, that union of God with humanity is what Christmas is all about. Advent counts down to that every year over the course of four Sundays. Advent points to that.

But there is more. There is something else that all the Advent calendars miss completely. Not only does Advent look forward to celebrating how God is united with us in the birth, life, and death of Jesus, but Advent also looks ahead to our being reunited. Advent is about union, and also about reunion. In his first letter to the church at Thessalonica, Saint Paul says how much he looks forward to being reunited with the people there. "Night and day, we pray most earnestly that we may see you face to face and restore whatever is lacking in your faith." That same letter goes on to talk about our reunion with our Lord on that day when he will come again.

Advent is a time of waiting — real waiting. There is more to it than just reenacting the long wait for the birth of the Messiah. In Advent, we are reminded that all of Christian life is waiting for Jesus to come again as he promised. In the Apostles' Creed, we distill to the bare bones what Christians believe about Jesus. It is hardly a complete list, but it is the essentials. Jesus is the Son of

God. Jesus is our Lord. He was conceived of the Holy Spirit, and the Virgin Mary gave birth to him. He suffered, he was crucified, he died, and he was buried. He went where the dead go. And then he rose. He came back to life. He rose up into heaven and took his seat at the Father's right hand. All of that happened a long time ago. All of that is the story of Christmas and Epiphany and Easter and the Ascension and everything else in between. And it is history; it is ancient history. All of that forever changed the way God interacts with the world. What follows is in our future. Jesus will come to judge the living and the dead. The Apostles' Creed speaks of what God did through Jesus in the past. It promises what God will do through Jesus in the future. But what about now?

After the phrase "and he is seated at the right hand of the Father", and before the mention of Christ's second coming, there is a comma. "He is seated at the right hand of the Father" "*comma*" "and he will come again to judge the living and the dead." Right there, in that comma, is where we are. That is our present. All of Christian history has happened in that comma. Nations and empires have risen and collapsed, entire languages have come and gone, the entire life of everyone we have every met has been lived in that comma. A period at the end of a sentence means that the statement is over. A comma means that there is more to come.

The kingdom of heaven is here, but there is more to come. Christ's love and peace and presence is seen in his people, but there is even more coming. Jesus is with us in everything; in the good times and the hard times, in our joy and in our times of panic, in our triumphs and in our suffering. But there is more to come. We still wait for that time Jesus will be with us more fully than we could ever imagine. We still wait for that time when suffering, loss, doubt, pain, sorrow, and separation will be no more.

Advent is a reminder of that waiting. It is a reminder that Jesus is always calling us forward. Jesus is calling us to grow in faith, and compassion and love. Jesus stands in the future with open arms. All of Christian life is waiting. All of Christian life is moving toward Jesus. All of Christian life is Advent.

Amen.

Second Sunday of Advent (SB)
Philippians 1:3-11

Life In The Future

I thank my God every time I remember you, constantly praying with joy in every one of my prayers for all of you, because of your sharing in the gospel from the first day until now. I am confident of this, that the one who began a good work among you will bring it to completion by the day of Jesus Christ.

It is right for me to think this way about all of you, because you hold me in your heart, for all of you share in God's grace with me, both in my imprisonment and in the defense and confirmation of the gospel. For God is my witness, how I long for all of you with the compassion of Christ Jesus. And this is my prayer, that your love may overflow more and more with knowledge and full insight to help you to determine what is best, so that in the day of Christ you may be pure and blameless, having produced the harvest of righteousness that comes through Jesus Christ for the glory and praise of God.

The earth revolves around the sun at a steady and predictable rate of about 67,000 miles per hour. We can count on that... and we do. The speed at which the earth orbits the sun is so reliable that we can set our calendars to it... and we do. We mark our calendars, keep our personal records, and schedule our lives based on it. We count our age and the age of everyone and everything we see by how many times we have ridden the earth around the sun. It is how we organize history. Every human culture there has ever been has ordered their lives around the repeating seasons of the year; around a predictable cycle of harvests and rainy seasons. For many people living now, changes in weather and the timing of agriculture don't play into their planning very much, but even for them, birthdays and anniversaries, holidays

Second Sunday of Advent

and commemorations are all linked to how long it takes the earth to make its 580,000,000 mile circuit around the sun.

The followers of Jesus have long had an annual pattern of holy days and celebrations: Christmas and Easter, Palm Sunday and Good Friday, Holy Trinity, Christ the King, All Saints' Day, Reformation Day, and many others. We call this the liturgical calendar, or more simply, the church year. The church year still takes up the same amount of time as it takes the earth to go 'round the sun. The church year is 365 days long, most of the time, with an extra day thrown in at leap year when there needs to be. There are however, some big differences between the church year and the solar year. To start with, instead of four seasons there are six, and they can be as short as twelve days and as long as six months. The seasons of the liturgical calendar are Advent, Christmas, Epiphany, Lent, Easter, and Pentecost. But the most important difference is that the church year isn't so much a matter of the earth revolving around the sun. The church year instead gives us a way to order our lives around Jesus. The seasons and holidays of the church and the stories that they tell take us through the whole life and ministry of Jesus, and through the story and teaching of the church. The church year starts off with anticipation, with waiting. It starts not with January, like our solar calendar does, but with Advent.

When you think about it, Advent is the perfect way to start off the church year, because Advent looks ahead. Advent is the season when we prepare to celebrate God becoming incarnate (literally "in the flesh") in the baby Jesus at Christmas. Advent is also a time to wait in joyful anticipation for the return of our Lord Jesus, when God will make all things new.

In the past half dozen decades or so, more and more congregations have adopted blue as the color associated with Advent. This is not simply a matter of decoration or style. Advent is all about expecting, hoping for, and counting on, what comes next. It is about the coming of Jesus into the world, first as a baby in a manger, and again, sometime in the future, when he will bring God's kingdom in all its fullness. Blue/violet represents

Down To Earth

Advent because is it the color of the morning sky. Blue is the color of the new day. It is the color of the future. Blue/violet is the color of what comes next.

We often worry about the future. It can be frightening because the future is so uncertain. We have no real way of knowing what is coming next. We so often wish that our current situations will pass and that life will return to the way it was. But history doesn't work that way. History may repeat itself at times, but it never moves backward. The future is always different from the present, and the present is different from the past. Always. That's the way that history works.

In the life of the church, it is so easy to long for the golden days gone by when things were, at least in our imaginations, more faithful, more secure, and just generally better. "If only" we say: "if only we could be the church that I remember from…" "If only we could go back to when…". But the Holy Spirit doesn't work that way either. God is not the God of the ideal. Jesus didn't wait until we got everything perfect to come among us. God doesn't wait for us to get there. God comes to us, whether we're ready or not. God comes to us as we are, and then moves us forward. The Holy Spirit moves, and the Holy Spirit moves us. The Holy Spirit never lets us remain stagnate. It takes us where we are, and moves us closer to God and closer to our neighbor. The Holy Spirit calls us, leads us, and when necessary, drags us out into the ever-changing world to show that world the love and hope and forgiveness of Jesus.

We don't know what the future holds, with a very important exception. The future has Jesus in it. The future holds Jesus. We can know that with absolute certainty. In the future, Christ will continue to be with us. Jesus is calling us into the future with him. The Holy Spirit is moving us into the future. There is one other thing that we can know for sure. The future has other people in it. We will not be alone. To carry on the work of Jesus, to show his love to the world, is not a solo project.

God could have stopped at Adam. God could have created just the one person and called it a day, but that is not what happened.

Second Sunday of Advent

God didn't just create a person. God created people. God created people to support each other, to care for each other and to love each other. God called, gathered, and enlightened the Christian church on earth. In hundreds of countries, through thousands of languages, across tens of thousands of denominations, God has formed the one church, the one body of Christ. You are God's gift to the world as a whole, and specifically to the other members of the body of Christ, and those countless members, scattered throughout time and space, are God's very real gift to you. Remember that this Advent. Remember that we are united by our baptism and made one by the work of the Holy Spirit. God made us to live together and to work together and to be God's people together. As we show God's love to the world, we do it together. As we serve God and our neighbor, we serve together. As we wait for our Lord to come again, we wait together.

Amen.

Third Sunday of Advent (SB)

Philippians 4:4-7

Don't Worry, Be Peaceful

Rejoice in the Lord always; again I will say, Rejoice. Let your gentleness be known to everyone. The Lord is near. Do not worry about anything, but in everything by prayer and supplication with thanksgiving let your requests be made known to God. And the peace of God, which surpasses all understanding, will guard your hearts and your minds in Christ Jesus.

We just want to know what comes next. We just want to know how things will turn out. Will we be safe? Will it be okay? What will the new baby be like? Who's going to win? Did you get the job? Will you get accepted? Will that special person say "yes"? Will they find a cure? Waiting for answers; having to sit by while the test results are taking forever; can be frustrating, scary, and almost painful. We really want to know. We need to know.

If we knew what was coming, we would know what to do to be ready for it. We would know how to brace for it. If we knew what was coming, we could take steps to prevent the bad and encourage the good. If we knew what was coming, we could have some control over it. When we don't know what will happen next, we are not in charge. We are not in control and we don't like it. We need to know.

On the fringes, there has always been a brisk business in fortune telling. Palm reading and dealing out Tarot cards aren't taken seriously by most people, but we're all a little intrigued. It's hard not to imagine that our minds would be just a little more at ease if we really could learn something from horoscopes and Ouija boards. Looking for ways to know the future is not limited to the occult and the ridiculous, however. Quite a bit of "mainstream" energy goes into trying to figure out what comes next. There are

Third Sunday of Advent

people whose full time job is to predict the weather. Millions of dollars of equipment and generations of computer programs have been developed to help them. There is an entire industry devoted to political polling aimed at predicting the outcome of elections. There are trailers to upcoming movies, and armies of fans who dissect and analyze those trailers for hidden hints of what will happen in the film.

A lot of this is simple curiosity. There is not much at stake in the real world when it comes to the plot of a popular movie series. The only thing at risk there is some temporary disappointment. But for things of real consequence, for times when everything rides on future events that we cannot foresee, what is really at play is worry. We worry that our medical test will give us answers we don't want. We worry that new political leadership will take us in dangerous directions. We worry about our friends and our family. We worry about war and disease and disaster. We worry that what we have can be taken away in an instant.

"Don't worry about anything." So says our second lesson for today from Saint Paul's letter to the church at Philippi. Don't worry about anything. How exactly is that supposed to work? You don't worry about things you don't care about. You don't worry if you aren't aware that any can go wrong. We all have plenty of things we don't worry about at all. But "don't worry about anything"? Anything? What about really important things? What about matters of life and death? Are we not supposed to care? Are we not supposed to pay attention?

History is full of religious and philosophical movements that have gone in that direction. They identify emotional attachment as the ultimate source of pain. If you don't bond with anyone or with anything, then you won't be hurt when those people leave, or when those things are taken away. If you don't care when have them, you won't care when they're gone. This, of course, is not at all what Jesus says. Jesus tells us to love our neighbors. Jesus says to pray for our enemies. Jesus says that everyone matters. What we do matters. What we opt not to do, and what we fail to do also matter. The gospel is that Jesus cares about us. Jesus cares about our lives. Jesus cares about us all. Jesus is attached. The baby in the manger is proof of that. The healing, teaching, and feeding that Jesus did among us is proof of that. His willingness to face a horrible death for us and his utter refusal to let death keep him away, are proof positive that Jesus cares. Jesus is attached to us. And through Jesus, God is attached to us.

Do not worry about anything, but in everything by prayer and supplication with thanksgiving let your requests be made known to God. And the peace of God, which surpasses all understanding, will guard your hearts and your minds in Christ Jesus.
(Philippians 4:6-7)

How can you not worry about things that matter? How can you not fear the loss of people, of things, of institutions that matter to you? How can you find peace when there is so much beyond your control; when there is so much that is uncertain?

We are deep into the season of Advent. Advent is a time of waiting. In Advent, we get ready to celebrate how God came to us at Christmas. We gear ourselves up to joy in the coming of Christ. There is more to our waiting however than just a countdown to Christmas. In Advent we don't just pretend to wait for something that happened millennia ago, and then feign surprise at the birth of Jesus. Advent is a time of real waiting. It is a time of real anticipation and expectation. It is a time to look toward what comes next. It is a time to look forward to the promised return of our Lord.

We all know the phrase "the peace which passes understanding." It is something that gets used in worship all the time. It is a peace that doesn't come from what we know, or what we can understand. It is a peace that comes in the face of uncertainty. It is a calmness, a gentleness, that cannot be chased off by the fear of the unknown. The peace the passes understanding is a gift that keeps worry at bay.

We do not know what will happen next. We cannot predict when tragedy or great fortune will come into our lives. Wars and sickness, new trends, and unforeseen technological innovations continue to surprise us. We can't see into the future — with one exception. We know that Jesus will come again. We know that no matter what happens, God is with us. We know that in all things and at all times, Jesus loves us and claims us as his own.

The peace of God does not come from what we know. The peace of God is beyond our understanding. The peace of God comes from trust in God's presence. The peace of God comes from faith in the words and works of Jesus. The peace of God comes from our Lord's promise of forgiveness and resurrection. The peace of God comes from hope.

Amen.

Fourth Sunday of Advent (SB)
Hebrews 10:5-10

Not A Religion

Consequently, when Christ came into the world, he said, "Sacrifices and offerings you have not desired, but a body you have prepared for me; in burnt offerings and sin offerings you have taken no pleasure.

Then I said, 'See, God, I have come to do your will, O God' (in the scroll of the book it is written of me)." When he said above, "You have neither desired nor taken pleasure in sacrifices and offerings and burnt offerings and sin offerings" (these are offered according to the law), then he added, "See, I have come to do your will." He abolishes the first in order to establish the second. And it is by God's will that we have been sanctified through the offering of the body of Jesus Christ once for all.

Every human culture there has ever been; any civilization, no matter how basic or how complex, always has a sense of the other. There is always an understanding that there is more to the world that we can see. There are things beyond our understanding. There are minds and wills and forces beyond us at work in the world and at work in our lives. In some cultures it is a god. Other times it could be a bunch of gods. It could be stars, planets, the moon, the spirits of ancestors, the trees and animals, or maybe the mind of the earth itself. Always there is something other. There is always something holy out there, beyond us and above us. This awareness of something powerful and unseen, something that gives purpose to our lives and makes sense of the world, is part of what it means to be human. There is more to it than that, however. It's not just that there is something holy out there, or up there, or deep within. There is within us a drive to connect with that something.

Religion is what we call our need to connect with that god,

Fourth Sunday of Advent

or those spirits. Religion is an attempt to transcend the physical world, and to contact the spiritual. Religion is a way to get to God. The word "religion" comes from the Latin word *religare*, which means "to tie back." Religions bind you to certain practices and traditions. Religions require you to hold back from certain behaviors. Often, religions seek to lead people to holiness by prescribing what they can and cannot eat, what they should wear, with whom they should associate, when and how they should pray. Religions often require sacrifices. They encourage and sometimes demand that people give up doing certain things or owning certain things or acting in certain ways in order to earn the protection and favor of whatever is "up there." In many religions, there are people set aside to act as go-betweens for God and humanity. They offer sacrifices to God (or the gods) on behalf of the people, and they speak for God to the people. In ancient Judaism, these people were called priests. Lots of religions have these mediators. They represent God to the people, and they represent the people to God.

Today is the last Sunday in the season of Advent. Before we move on to Christmas and Advent drops off of our radar for another year, there is something we need to look at. Advent isn't just a place-holder until Christmas comes. The season of Advent reveals an incredible secret about Christianity, a secret that we Christians ourselves so often miss. For four weeks we have looked ahead to celebrating how God came to us as a baby in a manger. For four weeks we have been looking ahead to the day when Jesus will return as he promised. Advent is about God coming to us. And there it is. That's the world shattering, mind-bending secret of Christianity: Christianity is not a religion!

At its heart, as it was given to us by Jesus and passed down through the first apostles, Christianity is not a religion. If anything, it is the very opposite of religion. Religions seek to take us beyond what we see. Religions provide ways for us to get to God. Christianity turns that completely upside down. Christianity isn't about us getting to God. The gospel is that in Jesus, God comes to us! God comes to us as a baby in a manger. God comes to us as a healer and a teacher. God comes to us as a man nailed to a cross. God comes to us out of the tomb, out of

Down To Earth

death. Religion tries to take us up to God. Christian faith is that God comes down to us.

Christian life is not about being good or being worthy so that we can get to God. It is about living in grace and forgiveness and peace because Jesus has already come to us. We don't make ourselves worthy of God's favor. Instead, the whole point of the Christian faith is that God's love makes us worthy. It is God who bridges the gap. It is God who crosses the distance. Our effort does not and cannot unite us with God. Only God can do that, and in Jesus, God does do that. Salvation is not our job. It's *way* above our paygrade. Salvation is God's job.

The second lesson for today is from the letter to the Hebrews in the New Testament. No one knows who wrote it, but it clearly comes from a time before 70 AD, when the temple in Jerusalem was destroyed by the Roman Empire. It was written at a time when Jewish priests were still offering burnt animal sacrifices to God. That was how it was done. It is what the Old Testament commanded. To people for whom their beloved and sacred, scriptural religious practices involved priests and sacrifices and the right way to do things, the author of the letter writes "Consequently, when Christ came into the world, he said, "Sacrifices and offerings you [God] have not desired, but a body you have prepared for me; in burnt offerings and sin offerings you have taken no pleasure." It's a radical, bold, challenging, and irreligious thing to say. The point is this: God comes to us. God comes to us and our salvation is not up to us, or our sacrifices or how well we follow the rules. Our salvation is in the hands of Jesus. Jesus is himself the sacrifice. Nothing else is needed. Jesus is the true and eternal, once and for all great high priest. There is no need for any middle-man. God comes to us in the flesh. God comes to us in the manger. God comes to us in death and God brings us to himself in resurrection.

As Advent ends for this year, remember that God has come to us in Jesus. Remember that we wait for Jesus to come and bring us the kingdom of heaven. Forgiveness has come to us. Love has come to us. Salvation is coming. Hope is coming. God is coming. Come, Lord Jesus!

Amen.

Nativity of Our Lord (SB)

Titus 3:4-7

But, Why?

But when the goodness and loving kindness of God our Savior appeared, he saved us, not because of any works of righteousness that we had done, but according to his mercy, through the water of rebirth and renewal by the Holy Spirit. This Spirit he poured out on us richly through Jesus Christ our Savior, so that, having been justified by his grace, we might become heirs according to the hope of eternal life.

Merry Christmas!

It's finally here! After counting down the school days and the work days, the shopping days and the paydays, it is finally Christmas. The shows and the songs and the parties, the holiday specials and the neighborhood lights and the door buster sales have all been leading to this. It is a happy day for most of us, a sad day for some of us, a stressful day for many and a big day for us all. Whether it warms your heart, boils your blood, or leaves you cold, Christmas has an impact on you.

The entire month of December seems to center around it, and for many businesses, it can make or break the whole fiscal year.

As Christian people, we see a little bit more when we look at Christmas. We see past the baking and decorating, past the crowded roads and stores, past the candy canes and inflatable snowmen, and the big expenses. As Christians we know what this holiday really is. We know that the Christmas light in this winter season has nothing to do with candles and strands of mini LED lights.

We know that God came to us through a young peasant girl and her trusting new husband. We know that the baby in a manger is so much more than six or seven pounds of bouncing Jewish baby boy. We know that the baby was also God in the flesh.

Down To Earth

We know that the infant Jesus is somehow the Word of God. We know that strangely, inexplicably, impossibly, the very creative power that brought the whole universe into existence lay on a pile of cow feed in the outskirts of Bethlehem, wearing a diaper. It's a mystery and a wonder that will never completely fit into our brains, but by faith we believe it to be true, comprehensible or not. As Christians, we know all of these deeper things about Christmas.

What we may not know is "why?"

Why would God leave the rarified glory of heaven to come to be among us? Why would the most holy one, who is beyond space and time and our imaginations, come to us and live in our dirty, earthy world? It doesn't really make sense. We talk about it like it's the most normal thing there is, that God would choose to live among us where there is hunger and pain, where this is joy and disappointment. We think of it as inevitable. We act as though it were logical for far off and powerful God to suddenly change tactics and close the distance between heaven and earth down to zero. But it's just not. It is neither logical, sensible, nor inevitable. Why did God choose to take flesh and live among us? This world is messy, and we are very far from perfect. Yes, we love, laugh, and write songs. We imagine, build, and occasionally do heroic, selfless things. But we also lie to each other and cheat each other. We argue, feud, and hold grudges. We discriminate and exclude. We rob, kill, and start wars. And yes, there is beauty in the world, and generosity. There is curiosity and sights to bring you to tears. But there are splinters here, and head colds. There is disease, drama, and dad-jokes. There is real tragedy. There is poverty. There is abuse. There is cruelty here, and death. So when we get to Christmas, when we get to the celebration of God's miraculous incarnation, it's a good and honest thing to scratch our heads and ask "Why?" Why would God do such a thing?

One thing is clear. God did not come to us in Jesus Christ because he had to. There is nobody or no thing that can force God to do anything. If there were, then we would call that thing God. God did not come to us in Jesus Christ out of obligation. God didn't owe us anything. It's not like humanity had anything on God, and God somehow had to pay off the debt.

So why did God come to us at Christmas? Why did the mind of infinity, the animating force of everything, the foundation of reality itself show up in our world and in our lives as a helpless newborn? It's actually pretty straightforward. God came to us in order to be with us. It's really that simple. God came to us to be close to us, to understand and unite with us. God came to us because God couldn't stay away. God came to his broken and imperfect world because he made it, loved it, and called it "very good." God was born among us to be among us. Jesus died to save us so that we would be saved. Jesus rose from the dead so that we could live with him. Why did God come to us? Why does God come to us now? Why is God with us in all that we go through? Because God loves us, pure and simple. God loves us. God made us, loves us, and calls us his very own. God cannot stay away.

So when you see your friends and family this Christmas, see the God who loves you. When you miss those long gone, see the God who longs for you. When you see the lights and the decorations, even when you see the candy canes and the inflatable snowmen, know that God chose to be in the world and in your life because God loves you. Know that God was born for you, lived for you, died for you, and rose for you. Know that God cannot bear to leave you. Know that God is always with you. Know that God loves you.

Merry Christmas!
Amen.

First Sunday after Christmas Day (SB)

Colossians 3:12-17

Put On Christ

As God's chosen ones, holy and beloved, clothe yourselves with compassion, kindness, humility, meekness, and patience. Bear with one another and, if anyone has a complaint against another, forgive each other; just as the Lord has forgiven you, so you also must forgive. Above all, clothe yourselves with love, which binds everything together in perfect harmony. And let the peace of Christ rule in your hearts, to which indeed you were called in the one body. And be thankful. Let the word of Christ dwell in you richly; teach and admonish one another in all wisdom; and with gratitude in your hearts sing psalms, hymns, and spiritual songs to God. And whatever you do, in word or deed, do everything in the name of the Lord Jesus, giving thanks to God the Father through him.

Merry Christmas!

Nearly every culture, nearly every religion has some kind of celebration in the winter. This stems, no doubt, from those times when months and months of short days and long nights, when water froze and no food could grow and exposure to the weather could cost you your life, made winter a real threat to survival. Winter festivals were a necessary lift to our collective spirits. Even now, when we have year-round food supplies and reliable heating, winter is much easier to bear when can we take time to celebrate, to pray, to give gifts and to get together with the important people in our lives. Christmas certainly serves this purpose. It is a highlight that comes at the darkest time of the year. These festival days exist to show us life in the dead of winter.

Maybe you got a new sweater this Christmas. You might have given someone gloves as a gift, or shoes, or a coat, or pajamas

First Sunday after Christmas Day

that match the rest of the family. Maybe you got underwear. Kids may feel let down, no matter how they might try and hide their disappointment, whenever the wrapping paper reveals a flat, non-rattling box of clothes, but most adults feel differently. Clothes can be practical and long lasting, or flashy and trendy. Clothes can make a statement, or they can help you to blend in. You can dress up, dress casual, dress for work, dress to impress, dress for success, and even dress to kill (figuratively, let's hope). Some people don't give a second thought to what they put on. Others may plan their wardrobes weeks in advance.

They say that "clothes make the person," and it's not entirely untrue. What you wear has a big influence on how people think of you and how they treat you. The style of your outfit can signal whether you are up to date or out of touch. How you are dressed can make the difference as to whether people listen to you or ignore you. A lab coat or a police uniform can communicate authority. Neat, professional clothes can send the message that you know what you are doing (even if you actually don't). Unclean, unkempt, or mismatched clothing can undermine your authority and silence your voice to others. What people see you wearing has a big impact on who people see you to be. What you clothe yourself with even shapes who you see yourself to be.

In Christian traditions where adult baptisms are the norm, the person being baptized often wears a white gown. When babies are baptized, their parents will sometimes wrap them up in a long and frilly white dress that has been passed through the family for generations. A few years later, those same parents might dress their child up in formal white clothes for the first time that child shares in Holy Communion. White robes normally cover the neatly tied neckties and carefully chosen outfits of confirmation students. Acolytes, communion assistants, lay readers, pastors and deacons also regularly put on white robes to lead worship. And when at the last, a coffin bears a dearly departed member of the body of Christ into the church's sanctuary for the last time, the casket itself is covered with a long white cloth. That cloth, called a funeral pall, serves the same purpose as those frilly white baby dresses, and the robes worn by confirmands and worship leaders. All of these things serve as a reminder of our baptism. We put them on to help us remember that baptism changes us. When we are clothed in baptism, we put on Christ. We wear the death and resurrection of Jesus. It covers us. It changes how the worlds sees us, how we look to our neighbors, and even how we understand ourselves. Baptism certainly changes how God sees us. When God looks at us, the first thing God sees is the love, forgiveness, and worthiness of Jesus that surrounds us like a garment. Clothes may not actually make the person, but baptism does.

Nearly every culture, nearly every religion has some kind of celebration in the winter. Christmas is more than this. It's more than just a morale booster; more than just a pick-me-up when the days are short and the skies are grey. Christmas isn't just another winter festival. It's not just another excuse for parties, gift exchanges, and lighting up the front of your house. Christmas is so much more. Christmas is about the miraculous, impossibly loving way that God came to us as a baby in a manger and quite literally put on our humanity. The baby wrapped in swaddling bands was God incarnate — God in the flesh. Christmas is about the one source and Creator of reality being wrapped up in a human body, a human life, and human history. At Christmas, God put on our humanity, and in our baptism, we are called to put on Christ.

"As God's chosen ones, holy and beloved, clothe yourselves with compassion, kindness, humility, meekness, and patience." (Colossians 3:12)

Maybe you didn't get a sweater this Christmas. Maybe there was no flat non-rattling box with something new for you to put on. But Christ has come to you. God has come to you. Jesus came thousands of years ago; and although he ascended into heaven way back in the far away reaches of ancient history, he remains with us now. God put on human life. God clothes himself with human joy and with human pain. God wore human anticipation and disappointment, wore our suffering and wore our death.

First Sunday after Christmas Day

Because God has come to us, because God became something different out of compassion and love for us, we too have been changed. In our baptism into the death and resurrection of our Lord, we have been given salvation to wear. We have been given hope to wear. Our baptism is a gift. Our life in Christ is a gift. Unwrap that gift. Unwrap it and put it on and parade around in it! Put on the gift of life. Put on the promise of resurrection. Put on compassion. Put on kindness and humility. Put on meekness and patience. Let the world see who Jesus has made you to be. Let the world look at you and see what Jesus has done and what Jesus is doing. Let the world look at you and see Jesus. Put on Christ!

Merry Christmas!

Amen.

New Year's Day (SB)
Revelation 21:1-6a

What's New?

Then I saw a new heaven and a new earth; for the first heaven and the first earth had passed away, and the sea was no more. And I saw the holy city, the new Jerusalem, coming down out of heaven from God, prepared as a bride adorned for her husband. And I heard a loud voice from the throne saying, "See, the home of God is among mortals. He will dwell with them as their God; they will be his peoples, and God himself will be with them; he will wipe every tear from their eyes. Death will be no more; mourning and crying and pain will be no more, for the first things have passed away." And the one who was seated on the throne said, "See, I am making all things new." Also he said, "Write this, for these words are trustworthy and true." Then he said to me, "It is done! I am the Alpha and the Omega, the beginning and the end. To the thirsty I will give water as a gift from the spring of the water of life.

It's a very common way that we greet one another. As soon as we get past the "hello" or "hey", we move onto half-rhetorical questions. It's mostly just a way to get the conversation going.

"So, what's new?" we ask. "What's new with you?" "What's up?"

Occasionally, we have a good answer to that. Occasionally we do have something genuinely new to report. It could be something positive; a new job, a new birth or marriage, an upcoming trip or a long awaited and long overdue recognition. Other times the news is unfortunate; a new sickness in the family, the death of a mutual acquaintance, a downturn in your personal circumstances. Most of the time, however, there really isn't a ready answer to those questions.

"What's new?" Often times nothing is new; not really; not

anything worth mentioning. Especially if you are talking to a person you see regularly, there is not likely to be any great earth shattering developments since you saw them last. More often than not, our answer to that question of what's new, is that there really isn't anything all that new. "Not much", we might say; "same old, same old." Most of the time, there is nothing new.

Yesterday was New Year's Eve. Yesterday was all about the countdown. Yesterday was all about the evening. As much as we might look forward to New Year's Eve, what we really celebrate is its ending. It's probably the only holiday where the real celebration breaks out only after it is over. Whether you stayed awake all the way to midnight, or you fell asleep hours before, last night had a certain finality to it. The purpose of New Year's Eve, it's primary job, is to end.

Today is New Year's Day. Today's purpose, it's primary job, is to start something new. Today is all about what is coming. Today is all about potential. Today we joy in speculation and probability and promise. Today looks ahead to an unknown future with optimism. We open new and empty calendars with hope. Anything can happen. Great things will happen this year, and terrible things too. Indelible memories will be made before our new calendars close for the last time, but many of the actual days in those calendars will blend blandly and forgettably together. All of it, the dramatic and the humdrum, brilliant and the boring, lies before us like a crisp napkin with no crumbs on it, like new snow without any footprints; fresh and new and unwritten. Today when we greet each other by asking "what's new", that question may not sound quite as cheap, not quite as perfunctory, not quite as meaningless as it did just yesterday. It might even get a little laugh out of us. "What's new?" Well, today at least, it feels like all of it is new.

Our second lesson today comes from the last pages of the Bible, from the penultimate chapter of the very last book. The setting is after the end of the world. The twenty-first chapter of the book of Revelation has a certain finality to it. The countdown has stopped and history is over. Here, a single page away from

Down To Earth

the back cover of holy scripture, we read these words of Saint John, the seer:

Then I saw a new heaven and a new earth; for the first heaven and the first earth had passed away, and the sea was no more. And I saw the holy city, the new Jerusalem, coming down out of heaven from God, prepared as a bride adorned for her husband. And I heard a loud voice from the throne saying, "See, the home of God is among mortals. He will dwell with them as their God; they will be his people, and God himself will be with them; he will wipe every tear from their eyes. Death will be no more; mourning and crying and pain will be no more, for the first things have passed away." And the one who was seated on the throne said, "See, I am making all things new."

Yes, this is clearly about the future. It addresses a time yet to come. For now, there are still tears. There is still mourning, crying, and pain. Death is very much part of the world we live in. The old things have not passed away, unfortunately. Grief, disaster, and tragedy are still very much alive and kicking. We are still counting down to that new day. And yet....

Today is New Year's Day. It is also the eighth day of Christmas. Christmas is about a new baby. It is about new parents. It is about new life and new family connections and a whole new start to the world. Christmas is about a new closeness between God and humanity. In Christmas, everything changes. God is no longer distant. God is no longer "up there."

God could easily have chosen to come down to us in Jesus and made everything perfect forever. God could have taken away mourning and pain and grief and death that Christmas morning slightly more than two thousand years ago. God could have, without doubt, have taken us out of the suffering that surrounds and defines us. There would be no need for the cross, no need for death, no need for resurrection. God instead chose to be with us in our suffering. In Jesus, God shared in our suffering, endured insult and injury and hatred, and even death. When God did that, all that stuff that defines us, mourning and crying and pain, were themselves redefined. In Christ, God makes all of human life sacred. Jesus makes all of human life holy. That's new. That's different. Because Jesus lived among us, and died for us, and rose for us, it's all good — even the bad stuff. All of our life right here, right now, is blessed, because Jesus is with us in all of it.

So, what's new? The answer is "everything." "See", says Jesus "I am making all things new." All things are new. Everything is new. Every year, every day, every hour, in the tiniest fraction of every second, Jesus is with us, making all things new.

Happy New Year!
Amen.

Second Sunday after Christmas Day (SB)

Ephesians 1:3-14

The Good Kind Of Awkward

Blessed be the God and Father of our Lord Jesus Christ, who has blessed us in Christ with every spiritual blessing in the heavenly places, just as he chose us in Christ before the foundation of the world to be holy and blameless before him in love. He destined us for adoption as his children through Jesus Christ, according to the good pleasure of his will, to the praise of his glorious grace that he freely bestowed on us in the Beloved. In him we have redemption through his blood, the forgiveness of our trespasses, according to the riches of his grace that he lavished on us. With all wisdom and insight he has made known to us the mystery of his will, according to his good pleasure that he set forth in Christ, as a plan for the fullness of time, to gather up all things in him, things in heaven and things on earth. In Christ we have also obtained an inheritance, having been destined according to the purpose of him who accomplishes all things according to his counsel and will, so that we, who were the first to set our hope on Christ, might live for the praise of his glory. In him you also, when you had heard the word of truth, the gospel of your salvation, and had believed in him, were marked with the seal of the promised Holy Spirit; this is the pledge of our inheritance toward redemption as God's own people, to the praise of his glory.

Merry Christmas!

It feels weird, doesn't it? It's technically correct to still say Merry Christmas. The Christmas Season is twelve days long — we know this because we sing it. It starts on December 25 and goes all the way until the January 5, so it is still Christmas. But once we get past New Year's Day and all the kids get ready to start back to school, it starts to feel a little strained to say "Merry Christmas." You might still have your Christmas tree up at home,

Second Sunday after Christmas

and all your decorations out and the outside lights still up, but that's all pretty well gone from stores, restaurants, and other public places. All the Christmas themed TV episodes and holiday specials have already aired. We won't be hearing "Rudolph, the Red Nosed Reindeer" and "Santa Baby" on the radio again until next November, or October, (or July,) or whenever it is they start playing that kind of stuff.

Try wishing a Merry Christmas to a stranger today when you're out in public, and you're likely to get stared at, and it's understandable. You might as well be wishing them a happy 4th of July. You'd sound like you don't know how to work a calendar. If you get any response at all to your cheerful "Merry Christmas", it's likely to be "Happy New Year". It's still technically Christmas, but talking about it now comes across as a little bit awkward.

Merry Christmas!

See? Awkward. And that's a very good thing.

Christmas parties can be a lot of fun. People going door-to-door singing carols is heartwarming. Displays of lights on a neighbor's front yard, or on street lamps down town brighten up a long dark winter evening far more than the few extra lumens they push out into the night. Candles, greeting cards, and the smell of cookies all give a warm and happy feeling to those last days of December. They also don't necessarily have anything to do with Jesus. That doesn't mean that any of these are problems, but rather that those things are enjoyable in their own right. You can have parties, cards, candles, and group singing at birthdays, or other celebrations.

When you talk about Christmas in January, you're not talking about snowmen and candy canes. People's minds have moved on from gingerbread and sleighs full of toys. Santa Claus is on sabbatical. The parties are over. The presents are all unwrapped, and some of them might even have been returned by now. It feels awkward to say "Merry Christmas" today because all of the holiday fluff is behind us. All of the things that the sales, the seasonal coffee flavors, and the holiday concerts have been leading up to are now more than a week in the past. If you refer to today, right here, right now, as Christmas, then you must not be talking about any of that stuff. If you really go through with the idea that today is still Christmas (and it is), then the only thing you can mean by the word "Christmas" is the celebration of the birth of Christ.

It may well be that today, the second Sunday in the season of Christmas, is the day when we can hear the message of Christmas the loudest and most clearly. Maybe it is only now, after the world has moved on and is gearing back up to business as usual, that those of us in the church — we who are the body of Christ, can feel how unusual, how life changing, the message of Christmas is.

Perhaps it takes this first Sunday of the new year to open our eyes to how new and how fresh the ancient nativity story really is.

Christmas is more than fun. It is more than heartwarming. Christmas goes well beyond a warm and happy feeling. Christmas changes everything. Christmas is the pivot that turns the whole of creation around. Christmas is about remembering that Jesus is in the world. Christmas is about the constant, loving, and very real presence of Jesus in our lives.

Everything changes because God is with us. Everything changes because God is here. The birth of Jesus changes the world; it changes our relationship with God, it changes how we deal with other people. Christmas marks that change. Because of Christmas, who we are responsible for and who we are responsible to is forever changed. Because of Christmas, the meaning of life will never be the same. Even the meaning of death has changed because of Christmas. Our success means something very different than it would without Jesus, and even our suffering has taken on a new and beautiful significance.

In our second lesson for today, from his letter to the Christian people in the ancient Greek city Ephesus, Saint Paul wrote:

God ... has blessed us in Christ with every spiritual blessing in the heavenly places, just as he chose us in Christ before the foundation of the world.... He destined us for adoption as his children through

Second Sunday after Christmas

Jesus Christ.... In him we have redemption through his blood, the forgiveness of our trespasses, according to the riches of his grace that he lavished on us.

Without Jesus, God is an abstraction, a far off force of life in the universe. But we are not without Jesus; God is real and God cares about what we do, who we are, and where we are in our lives. Without Jesus, our faith is a warm and happy, vague spiritual feeling. But we are not without Jesus. Jesus was born among us. Jesus lived our life. Jesus endured our suffering, and Jesus died our death. We are not without Jesus. Our faith in Jesus connects us to God. Our faith in Jesus connects us to his birth, life, suffering, and death. Our faith in Jesus binds us to his resurrection and to the life he gives forever. Our faith in Jesus makes God's children.

Christmas changes everything. Carry this hope into the new year. Bear the Christmas message into every corner, every second of your life. Take the good news of Jesus out into the world.

Merry Christmas!

Amen.

Epiphany of Our Lord (SB)

Ephesians 3:1-12

"Aha" Moment

This is the reason that I, Paul, am a prisoner for Christ Jesus for the sake of you Gentiles — for surely you have already heard of the commission of God's grace that was given me for you, and how the mystery was made known to me by revelation, as I wrote above in a few words, a reading of which will enable you to perceive my understanding of the mystery of Christ. In former generations this mystery was not made known to humankind, as it has now been revealed to his holy apostles and prophets by the Spirit: that is, the Gentiles have become fellow heirs, members of the same body, and sharers in the promise in Christ Jesus through the gospel. Of this gospel I have become a servant according to the gift of God's grace that was given me by the working of his power. Although I am the very least of all the saints, this grace was given to me to bring to the Gentiles the news of the boundless riches of Christ, and to make everyone see what is the plan of the mystery hidden for ages in God who created all things; so that through the church the wisdom of God in its rich variety might now be made known to the rulers and authorities in the heavenly places. This was in accordance with the eternal purpose that he has carried out in Christ Jesus our Lord, in whom we have access to God in boldness and confidence through faith in him.

The Greek mathematician and engineer Archimedes, who lived in the third century before Christ, was once given the job of determining whether a ceremonial crown presented to the king of Syracuse was really pure gold, as it was said to be. The tricky part was, he could do nothing that would harm the crown. None of his testing could leave even a scratch. This stumped him for quite a while. The story goes that one day, while Archimedes was

Epiphany of the Lord

getting into an overly full bathtub, the solution to his problem hit him like a flash. As he got into the tub, water overflowed the sides and spilled out onto the floor. The answer to his problem was to determine the density of the crown by dropping it into a full bowl of water, and measuring how much water spilled out. Then he would compare that amount to how much water was displaced by pure gold that weighed the same as the crown. If the crown displaced as much water as the gold, then it had the same density as gold. And if it had the same density as pure gold, then the crown itself was pure gold. It was a stroke of pure genius. Excited by his sudden lightning bolt of understanding, Archimedes leapt out of the bath and ran through town shouting 'Eureka, Eureka!' In Greek, that means 'I found it, I found it!'

Sometimes they call it an "aha" moment; a sudden burst of insight when everything comes together and it all makes sense. In cartoons, a light bulb will appear over a character's head to show that they now get it. Eureka! The answer to what had puzzled them for so long is now crystal clear. It's an abrupt dawning of comprehension. In Germany they say *"es geht ein Licht auf"*, which means "a light goes on". The Greek word meaning "to shine upon" comes down to us in English as a word that means a sudden revelation, an "aha" moment. That English word is "epiphany".

Today is the church holiday of Epiphany. In many parts of the world, they call it "Three Kings Day". Epiphany celebrates the arrival of "wise men" from the east (the Bible never says that they were kings, and it doesn't say how many there were, and it certainly doesn't give their names). The wise men, however many there were, took the shining light of a new star as a sign that something big was happening in Israel. A combination of arduous travel, knowing where to ask questions, and some more star gazing led them to the child who was God in the world. The shining of a star, and more importantly, what that star shined upon, was like a light bulb above a cartoon character's head. A light went on, literally in this case, and it showed them the Son of God. No doubt they said "aha" or "eureka" or whatever you

Down To Earth

would say in whatever language they spoke. They got it. They understood.

In the coming weeks, we will be reading stories from scripture that shine a light on who Jesus was, and who Jesus is, and what Jesus means in our lives. The season of Epiphany will conclude with the story of the transfiguration, when Jesus is shown in the bright light of God's glory, as the fulfillment and goal of the whole Old Testament, the ancient scripture passed forward from the prophets and priests of Israel.

Our second lesson today alludes to another epiphany story. St. Paul refers to his own experience of Jesus being made known to him. *"for surely you have already heard of the commission of God's grace that was given me for you, and how the mystery was made known to me by revelation, as I wrote above in a few words, a reading of which will enable you to perceive my understanding of the mystery of Christ."*

Paul was a rabbi and a leader in a theologically conservative Jewish group called the Pharisees - sort of. That description rather undersells the Pharisees. The truth is that these guys were hard core. The Pharisees followed the commandments in the Old Testament strictly — rigidly — rigorously. It's like they read through the Bible with a microscope, just looking for more rules to follow. They found them, too — loads of them. If you ask most people today how many commandments there are in the Old Testament, they would tell you that there are ten. The Pharisees found 613 commandments, and they followed them all. They followed them all, and they weren't shy about letting people know they followed them all, and they didn't hold back from condemning people who didn't follow them all. Chief among those who didn't follow the rules, in the eyes of the Pharisees, were the first followers of Jesus. As far as the Pharisees were concerned, Christianity was a misguided excuse for neglecting the laws of God. Paul bought into this big-time. It was Paul who gave the stamp of approval when the Deacon Stephen was stoned to death for telling people about Jesus. Paul later would go town to town to arrest people who followed Christ. When Paul was going to Damascus with his official written orders and his armed guards to round up Christians, he had an encounter that not only changed his own life forever, but also changed the course of human history. In all likelihood, it has even changed you.

As Paul neared Damascus, he had an epiphany. A light shined upon him. A bright light flashed and a voice said, "Why are you persecuting me? It was the voice of Jesus calling to him. It was the light of Christ shining upon him. This encounter with the light of Christ plunged Paul, who was still trying to rid the world of the followers of Jesus, into a sudden and literal darkness. He was temporarily struck blind. Paul had to be led into Damascus by the hand. Three days later, he met up with the Christians there as the voice had told him to do. When Paul did, the blindness fell off his eyes like pitch black contact lenses being removed. When he could see again, it wasn't even remotely the same. He had been enlightened all the way down to his toes. The light was too bright for condemnation or for self-righteousness. Paul saw past the rules and the commandments. He saw the world around him by the light of Jesus. Paul saw forgiveness. He saw the love of Jesus surrounding and available to everyone. He saw hope even where there was tragedy and disappointment. Paul spent the rest of his life traveling the known world and helping people to live in the light of Jesus. Through his letters in the New Testament, Paul has been shining the light of Jesus for nearly two thousand years.

What about you? It is unlikely that God showed you Jesus in the twinkling of a new star. That's not the way it happens most of the time. You probably didn't come to faith when the voice of Jesus accused you of persecuting God's people, and then rendered you temporarily blind. Chances are pretty strong that your own epiphany, your personal "aha moment" was significantly less dramatic. You might not be even able to point to any single moment, any specific event when the truth of the gospel became obvious to you, and clear, and compelling. You might be someone who can indeed circle a specific date on the calendar as the day you first realized that Jesus is your Lord and Savior.

Either way, the Holy Spirit is working in you, calling you,

making you holy, and enlightening you. You wouldn't be listening to this sermon; you wouldn't be here in worship, if that weren't absolutely true. Christ had been made known to you in your baptism, through the words of Paul, or other Christians. Somehow, a light went on, and you saw Jesus. You were given an epiphany. Eureka! Live in that light. See by that light. See the forgiveness, the hope, the opportunity and forgiveness that radiates outward from the cross of Jesus.

Light is the fastest thing we know about. Light never stays put. If there is light at all, that light is moving. The light that shines on you doesn't just come to you and stop. The light that shines on you keeps moving. Reflect the light of Christ so that it shines out into the world around you.

Amen.

Baptism of Our Lord/First Sunday after the Epiphany (SB)

Acts 8:14-17

But, What Does It Do?

Now when the apostles at Jerusalem heard that Samaria had accepted the word of God, they sent Peter and John to them. The two went down and prayed for them that they might receive the Holy Spirit (for as yet the Spirit had not come upon any of them; they had only been baptized in the name of the Lord Jesus). Then Peter and John laid their hands on them, and they received the Holy Spirit.

So, what is it, really, this Holy Spirit? What is it for? What does it do?

God the Father is understandable, even if we can't see him. People all have experience with fathers, or with father figures of some sort. We know about fathers. And even if our own experience with fathers is less than perfect — even if it is downright horrific, we know what a father should be. We have an ideal image of a father and of fatherly love. It is readily understood that when we call God *Father*, we have this ideal in mind. We get God the *father*. It is an ancient metaphor that still works.

God the Son is even easier. Jesus is God in the flesh: God literally down to earth. We may not have ever seen Jesus face-to-face, but lots of real people did. Countless thousands of people had the chance in Jesus to look God right in the eyes, to hear his voice, and to get his attention. Jesus is God in the simplest, most direct, least abstract form possible. Jesus wasn't a concept, or an underlying force, or loving feeling. Jesus was a guy. He had a face, a haircut, and a certain way of walking that his friends could recognize from a distance. You could go right up to Jesus and shake his hand. He had actual dirt under his actual fingernails. God we get. The Son of God we get. But the Holy Spirit?

First off, the name is confusing. Spirit is the word we use for

Down To Earth

the feeling of optimistic devotion that high school pep rallies are designed to inspire. Spirit is also the word we use for a person's soul, their inner life. A spirit can be a ghost. Older translations of the Bible call the Holy Spirit just that — the Holy Ghost. Is the Holy Spirit a phantom? A specter? Is it God's soul? The original Greek word that is translated as Spirit can also mean "breath" or even "wind". If anything, that makes the whole thing even less clear. Why don't we say Holy Breath? Why isn't it Father, Son, and Holy Wind? What really is the Holy Spirit?

We know what the Father does. God the Father creates. God the Father makes stuff. He makes everything from gravity to speed to covalent bonds. The Father makes quarks, quanta, and quasars; he also made oak trees, sloths, and your Uncle Larry. We know what God the Father does.

We know what the Son does. Jesus taught and healed. He suffered, died, and was buried. He rose from the dead, taught a little bit more, ascended into heaven, and promised to come again. Everything that that Bible tells us that Jesus did, every single word he has been quoted as saying, have been presented to us over the centuries on canvas, in marble and stained glass, in overly pious movies and Vacation Bible School songs. We know very, very well, what God the Son has done.

What about God the Holy Spirit? What is it and what does it do? We shouldn't feel guilty or inadequate if we don't have a quick and decent answer. Some of the very earliest Christians don't seem to have known much about it either. In our second lesson for today, from Acts 8, we hear:

"Now when the apostles at Jerusalem heard that Samaria had accepted the word of God, they sent Peter and John to them. The two went down and prayed for them that they might receive the Holy Spirit (for as yet the Spirit had not come upon any of them; they had only been baptized in the name of the Lord Jesus)".

Many chapters later, in Acts 19, Paul traveled to Ephesus and questioned baptized Christians he found there, who admitted that hadn't even heard that there *was* a Holy Spirit. So, what is it? Let's start with what it isn't. It isn't magic. It isn't a super-

Baptism of the Lord / First Sunday after the Epiphany

power. The Holy Spirit is not something you can take to get supernatural abilities or the power to predict the future. What the Holy Spirit is, is God. It is one of the three persons of the Holy Trinity. Christian baptism is done in the name of the Father and of the Son and of the Holy Spirit. If God the Father is the one who speaks reality into being (Genesis 1), and God the Son is the creative Word which the Father speaks (John 1), then the Holy Spirit is God's voice. The Holy Spirit is God active in the hearts, minds, and imaginations of the body of Christ, the church. What does the Holy Spirit do? In the words of Martin Luther, it "calls, gathers, and makes holy the whole Christian church on earth." The Holy Spirit is the source of faith. It gives us the faith we need as individuals to believe in the reality of God and the unlikely truth of the resurrection of Jesus, and it gives the faith that binds God's people together into the church, the body of Christ. The Holy Spirit calls us into the church, and the Holy Spirit sends us out into the world.

We say that we are made right before God by faith in Jesus Christ; that it is God's work alone, not ours, that saves us. That's pretty much the very core of what is it means to be Christian. God doesn't love us because we deserve to be loved, but because Jesus died and rose for us. God doesn't owe us anything, but rather God gives us everything out of mercy and grace. The shorthand we use for this is 'Justification by Faith'. Think of 'justify' in the sense we use it when writing. When we 'justify' the margins of the text we are writing, we line them up. The beginning of each line of words starts (or stops, or both) the same distance from the edge of the paper as the line above and below it, forming a straight line. When we are justified to God, we are lined up with God's will. We are made perfect in God's eyes. This is clearly not something that we can pull off by our own effort. We can't do it, so God does it. We are not justified by anything that we do, but only by faith in what Jesus has done.

"But" you may point out, "But isn't having faith still something we have to do?" Isn't it still up to us in that way? It would be, if faith was something that came from our heads, or from our hearts, or wills, or imaginations. Having faith would count as us doing something if faith were something that we did; if faith was something that we made. But we don't produce faith. We don't conjure up faith. We don't make faith; God makes faith. It is a gift given to us by the Holy Spirit. Yes, even our own faith is a gift from God.

We are baptized in the name of the Father, and of the Son, and of the Holy Spirit. God the Father creates us and all that there is. God the Son became one of us, lived with us, died to forgive us. God the Holy Spirit makes us able to believe that. The Holy Spirit makes us able to care. The Holy Spirit inspires us to live out our baptism every day in all that we do. In baptism, God the father makes us new. In baptism, the ancient story of the death and resurrection of God the Son becomes our personal story here and now. In baptism, God the Holy Spirit brings us faith and calls us to follow.

You are baptized in the name of the Father, and of the Son, and of the Holy Spirit. You are forgiven and loved in the name of the Father, and of the Son, and of the Holy Spirit. You are sent out into the world to make a difference in the name of the Father, and of the Son, and of the Holy Spirit. That's what God does, and how God does it through you.

Amen.

Second Sunday after the Epiphany (SB)

1 Corinthians 12:1-11

Gifted

Now concerning spiritual gifts, brothers and sisters, I do not want you to be uninformed. You know that when you were pagans, you were enticed and led astray to idols that could not speak. Therefore I want you to understand that no one speaking by the Spirit of God ever says "Let Jesus be cursed!" and no one can say "Jesus is Lord" except by the Holy Spirit. Now there are varieties of gifts, but the same Spirit; and there are varieties of services, but the same Lord; and there are varieties of activities, but it is the same God who activates all of them in everyone. To each is given the manifestation of the Spirit for the common good. To one is given through the Spirit the utterance of wisdom, and to another the utterance of knowledge according to the same Spirit, to another faith by the same Spirit, to another gifts of healing by the one Spirit, to another the working of miracles, to another prophecy, to another the discernment of spirits, to another various kinds of tongues, to another the interpretation of tongues. All these are activated by one and the same Spirit, who allots to each one individually just as the Spirit chooses.

What do we mean when we say that someone is gifted? If someone is unusually smart, or if they are a great singer, or a champion athlete, we might say they are gifted. A person who excels at playing the ukulele or at doing algebra in their head might be called gifted. It's a term we use for such a huge variety or skills and abilities, that it can be hard to say exactly what we mean when we say it. If a person who can tell you exactly what's wrong with your Chevy simply by hearing it start, and someone who can get a group of strangers together to cheerily and effectively get the job done are both gifted, then what really do we mean when we say that someone is gifted? Does it mean that they're good at doing a particular thing? Yes. Does it mean that they have just the right personality, just the right physical traits, just the right combination of interest, passion, and drive that sets them up to excel? Yes. It means all of those things, and underneath it all, it means something even more basic. When we call someone gifted, we are saying, quite literally, that they have been given a gift. It's really that simple. We are saying that the abilities, the drive, the personality traits, and the physical attributes that enable them to do so well, have been given to them. Calling someone gifted doesn't say so much about what their abilities are, or even how far those abilities go, as it is a statement about just where those talents came from. If you make something for yourself, it's not a gift to you. If you buy something for yourself, it's hardly a gift. If you earn something, if you deserve it, then that thing is not a gift to you. Gifts, by definition, are things that are given. Anything you buy for yourself, or earn or make for yourself is not a gift, because you're not giving it to anybody. A gift is a thing you give away. A gift is a thing that is given to you.

This is obvious, of course, but we so often overlook this clear and simple meaning when we call someone gifted. When we say that, we are not talking about how great that person is, or how accomplished, or even how deserving they are, but rather that what they can do, or how they act, or whatever it is that we admire about them was first given to them — by someone else. The lion's share of the praise and respect that these gifts inspire is properly directed to the source of those gifts. Listen to what you're really hearing when someone calls you gifted. Think about what you are really saying when you say that someone has a gift. As people of faith, let us never forget that if someone has what we would call a gift, that they didn't make it, earn it, or even deserve it. As people of faith, let us be aware that every good and perfect gift comes from the God who made us. Our bodies and minds, our abilities and interests, our passions and our drives have all come from God who created us. We did not create ourselves, God created us. We did not invent the things that go into making us who we are, all of it is gift.

Second Sunday after the Epiphany

In our second lesson today, Saint Paul listed nine spiritual gifts. They were: the utterance of wisdom, the utterance of knowledge, faith, gifts of healing, working of miracles, prophecy, the discernment of spirits, various kinds of tongues, and the interpretation of tongues. Some of them are the kind of abilities that some people just naturally exhibit. They are the kind of thing you might just have a knack for, like knowing useful things, or making inspiring and insightful statements. But most of the nine things listed here (let's be honest) are pretty exotic. A "gift of healing", unless you mean people in the medical field, certainly qualifies as unusual at least. "Miracle working" and "prophecy" are met by most people with a healthy and completely appropriate dose of skepticism. Most of us don't realistically expect to ever encounter the genuine articles. And while there are some Christian traditions where "speaking in tongues" and the "interpretation of tongues" are fairly commonplace, those things remain well beyond the experience of the vast majority of Christians. There is one thing on that list however that Christians of all kinds are familiar with. That one thing is "faith". Not only do all Christians know and use the word "faith," but all Christians agree as to how important it is. That's really saying something, as there are *very* few things that you can get all Christians to agree on. What makes "faith" stand out among the things on Saint Paul's list of spiritual gifts here in 1 Corinthians is not that it's unusual or exotic or even especially supernatural. Faith jumps out at you in this list because we don't generally think of it as a gift.

It's not just that we as individuals fail to recognize where faith comes from. The whole church itself has been accidentally and inadvertently misleading people by saying over and over again (especially during the last half millennium) that we are saved by faith. This is certainly not untrue, but it's not the whole thing either. Saying that you are saved by faith, and stopping at that, can sound like you are saying that you are saved by belief, or by conviction, or by you own will power. We are not, in fact, made right by God by certainty or be any mental process of our own. We are made right by God by the death and resurrection of Jesus.

Down To Earth

We are justified by faith *in Jesus*. Faith only saves us when it takes us beyond self-reliance and on to dependence on the grace of God shown to us in Jesus. We don't create the faith that lets us believe in Jesus. We don't dream up our own trust in God. We cannot buy nor can we earn the ability to see God at work in the world. We cannot talk ourselves (or anyone else) into loving Jesus. Our faith is not a product of our willpower. It is not our decision. Our faith was given to us. Our faith is a gift.

If you believe in God, you are gifted with faith. If you trust in Jesus, you are gifted. If you strive to love the Lord with all your heart, and mind, and strength, it is because you have been given the gift of faith. Even if you don't always do a very good job of loving God and neighbor, your desire to do better is a gift.

Maybe you can speak words of wisdom. Maybe you know lots of useful things. Maybe you speak in tongues or understand it when someone else is speaking in tongues. Maybe you do even have the gift of healing, or miracle working, or prophecy. You might be really good at math, organization, or at playing the ukulele. If you do, then you have a gift from God. Unwrap those gifts and put them use for the glory of God. Don't worry about overusing them. It's not like you'll ever wear them out. And beneath all that, underlying everything else, you have been given the gift of faith in Jesus. You have been given the gift that connects you in trust and in hope to the death and resurrection of your Lord. Faith is a gift. Use that gift. Live that gift. Show that gift. You'll never wear it out, but it wouldn't hurt to try.

Amen.

Third Sunday after the Epiphany (SB)
1 Corinthians 12:12-31a

Parts Is Parts

For just as the body is one and has many members, and all the members of the body, though many, are one body, so it is with Christ. For in the one Spirit we were all baptized into one body — Jews or Greeks, slaves or free — and we were all made to drink of one Spirit. Indeed, the body does not consist of one member but of many. If the foot would say, "Because I am not a hand, I do not belong to the body," that would not make it any less a part of the body. And if the ear would say, "Because I am not an eye, I do not belong to the body," that would not make it any less a part of the body. If the whole body were an eye, where would the hearing be? If the whole body were hearing, where would the sense of smell be? But as it is, God arranged the members in the body, each one of them, as he chose. If all were a single member, where would the body be? As it is, there are many members, yet one body. The eye cannot say to the hand, "I have no need of you," nor again the head to the feet, "I have no need of you." On the contrary, the members of the body that seem to be weaker are indispensable, and those members of the body that we think less honorable we clothe with greater honor, and our less respectable members are treated with greater respect; whereas our more respectable members do not need this. But God has so arranged the body, giving the greater honor to the inferior member, that there may be no dissension within the body, but the members may have the same care for one another. If one member suffers, all suffer together with it; if one member is honored, all rejoice together with it.

Now you are the body of Christ and individually members of it. And God has appointed in the church first apostles, second prophets, third teachers; then deeds of power, then gifts of healing, forms of assistance,

Down To Earth

forms of leadership, various kinds of tongues. Are all apostles? Are all prophets? Are all teachers? Do all work miracles? Do all possess gifts of healing? Do all speak in tongues? Do all interpret? But strive for the greater gifts.

They say that no two people are alike. Even each identical twin has a unique personality and a unique set of fingerprints. There is no one exactly like you, but there are people who are similar enough to you in some respects at least, that you feel you can really relate to them. There are others with whom you have little if any common ground. It can be hard to understand someone like that. The more things that are different, the harder it is to put yourself in someone else's shoes, and to imagine how the world must look through their eyes. People are different. It's just a fact of life. People talk differently from each other; they have different dialects and different languages. They reason differently. They think differently. They look different. They hold different opinions and have different ways of seeing the world. They have different abilities, different interests, and value different things.

We figure this out pretty early in life, but it never fully seems to sink in. That moment of surprise, or occasionally even shock can still sneak up on us when we encounter customs of ideas or ways of living that are completely alien to our own. Our reactions can range from innocent curiosity ("Huh, I never would have thought of that"), to puzzlement ("Why would anybody want to do that?") to disgust ("What is wrong with them?"), to outrage ("How could anybody ever think that is okay?"). Now, there are certain behaviors and certain opinions that are objectively immoral, hateful, and beyond the pale. But how quick we can be to condemn and to judge anything that goes up against the way we think, act, and conduct ourselves in the world. Rather than just acknowledging the differences we encounter, learning from them, or even embracing them, we all too often let difference become division.

We are divided by nationality. We are divided by politics. We are divided by generation and by gender and by race. We

Third Sunday after the Epiphany

are even divided over whether generation, race, and gender are real things, or mere imaginary social constructs. And while it might be easy for those of us in the church to imagine that such separations only happen in the world around us, the truth is less kind than that.

The church is very divided. We agree on the single most important things — that Jesus is Lord, that he is somehow God in the flesh, that he died for our sin and that he rose to give us forgiveness and life. Once you get past those things, however, we are split on nearly every issue you can think of. We are divided over the answers to questions vital to what it means to be Christian. How do you read the Bible? Is it literal history, or is it metaphor, or is it some mix of the two? What does baptism do for us, and who should be baptized? What happens when you take Holy Communion? How often should you take it? Is there a minimum age? Does is really have to be grape wine with an alcohol content and wheat based bread? Is a professional clergy really necessary? If so, who can they be? What is their authority? We are also deeply divided by things that are simply not important enough to cause arguments, but do anyways. What language can you pray in? Is there one correct translation of the Bible? What kind of music should you have in church? Can you use musical instruments? What kind of musical instruments? Can you have statues in your sanctuary? Paintings? Stained glass? Do you stand for worship? Sit? Is there a time to kneel? Should you genuflect? The list can go on pretty much forever. It's way too easy in the church at large, and in the pews on Sunday morning, to be distracted by the ways that our fellow worshipers are different from us. It is way too easy to imagine that since they are not the same as us, that they must be less devoted, less faithful, less serious, and simply less right than we are.

Here's what we tend to miss. Difference among people is not necessarily proof that everyone else is somehow defective. Christians who don't agree with you on what worship should look like or how the pastor should be dressed, or even how the Bible should be read may not be any less right than you are. They may not be any more wrong than you are. Difference between cultures, denominations, and individuals might well be instead an indication of something important and wonderful and very, very big. Our creative God makes each of us different, so that he can love each of us for who we are. Difference among people is evidence of God's enormous creativity. Much of the reason that we are different from each other is that God made us different from each other. God did not divide us — that is our own contribution. Human sin divides us. God made us different so that we can contribute to each other, so that we can supplement each other, and so that together we can be more than any of us could be alone.

"For just as the body is one and has many members", says Saint Paul to the church at Corinth, "and all the members of the body, though many, are one body, so it is with Christ." The congregation at Corinth was divided and needed to be reminded of exactly what it means to be the Body of Christ. If the church is the Body of Christ, then we should expect that the members of the church will serve different functions. A body is made of all kinds organs, nerves, bones, and other stuff. All of those parts do their own jobs, and all of those jobs together make the body work. If all the parts of a body were the same, then that body would die.

The eye can't say to the hand, "too bad you're not an eye, I guess that makes you useless". If you were just one big eyeball, how would you hear anything? If we consisted only of noses, or of gall bladders, how would we get anywhere? Every part of your body serves a purpose, (with the possible exception of the appendix) and you are best served having all of the parts, and having all of them working together.

We're not all the same, but God loves, redeems, and claims us all. We have different gifts and abilities, but there is no room for resentment or jealousy or looking down your nose at anyone. God calls us all together. We are all forgiven through the cross of Christ. We are all made alive by the resurrection of our Lord. We are all loved. We are all needed. God sends us out into the world to share life, mercy, and hope. No two people are alike, but in Jesus, we are all one.

Amen.

Fourth Sunday after the Epiphany (KvD)
1 Corinthians 13:1-13

Who's Love?

If I speak in the tongues of mortals and of angels, but do not have love, I am a noisy gong or a clanging cymbal. And if I have prophetic powers, and understand all mysteries and all knowledge, and if I have all faith, so as to remove mountains, but do not have love, I am nothing. If I give away all my possessions, and if I hand over my body so that I may boast, but do not have love, I gain nothing.

Love is patient; love is kind; love is not envious or boastful or arrogant or rude. It does not insist on its own way; it is not irritable or resentful; it does not rejoice in wrong doing, but rejoices in the truth. It bears all things, believes all things, hopes all things, endures all things.

Love never ends. But as for prophecies, they will come to an end; as for tongues, they will cease; as for knowledge, it will come to an end. For we know only in part, and we prophesy only in part; but when the complete comes, the partial will come to an end. When I was a child, I spoke like a child, I thought like a child, I reasoned like a child; when I became an adult, I put an end to childish ways. For now we see in a mirror, dimly, but then we will see face to face. Now I know only in part; then I will know fully, even as I have been fully known. And now faith, hope, and love abide, these three; and the greatest of these is love.

Some years ago I was in a Bible study focusing on faith in daily life. One of the passages we focused on was the one from 1 Corinthians 13, the famous passage on love, often read at weddings. But 1 Corinthians 13 is not about a wedding, but about our life as the body of Christ. The little church to whom Saint Paul wrote had been engaged in some pretty serious competition about who had the best spiritual gifts and he had a more excellent way in mind — the way of love.

But our association of this passage makes it hard for us to take in Saint Paul's meaning. The Bible study leader recommended this exercise: Reread the passage, taking "love" and substitute your name, and meditate on what you hear and try to live it out for a while.

I tried to live with that for a week, and I learned two things. First, it's a beautiful exercise in just how many opportunities we have to live in love. Second, for all the opportunities, living in love isn't so easy for us.

Think of it! "I am patient. I am kind. I am not envious, boastful, arrogant, or rude. I do not insist on my own way; I am not irritable or resentful; I do not rejoice in wrongdoing, but I rejoice in the truth." If you try to think in these terms, writing an email can become an opportunity for practicing kindness. Conversations among friends become opportunities to rejoice in what's good about people, rather than gossiping and griping. Julian of Norwich, a thirteenth-century saint and mystic, once had a vision of all of creation as the size of a hazelnut. Everything large is small enough to be loved, everything small is large enough to be loved. There are no details too trifling to be away from God's loving gaze and no agendas too large to be contained. Every moment is holy and every person someone to be loved!

"I am patient. I am kind. I am not envious, boastful, arrogant, or rude. I do not insist on my own way; I am not irritable or resentful."

But then, for what seems like the four hundredth time, someone calls and asks to speak to the person in charge of the electric bill, and there goes not being rude.

A friend posts her pictures on Facebook of her family heading down to Key West in January, and they all look so wonderful. Their family is intact. They are smiling. They are having a good time. They seem to have no dysfunctions or hidden dramas; they have no hurts. They are in the sun. In January! So much for not being envious.

Fourth Sunday after the Epiphany

An argument in your household about how to spend the next holiday turns into a fight that drags out for days. So much for patience, kindness, and not insisting in your own way.

The greatest commandment, Jesus said, was to love the Lord our God with all our heart, mind, and strength, and a close second is to love our neighbors as ourselves. God is most interested in this particular power, this ability: to love. Love is not a power that possesses or shows off or performs. Rather, love gives. Love confers good on others and in this way it puts every other gift, skill, or ability into proper perspective. We could speak like angels or sing like the Mormon Tabernacle Choir, but if we just do it for show and do not have love in our hearts, we might as well be banging pots and pans. If we have all kinds of skills and knowledge so as to build houses, or make crafts or lead classes, but if we see the less skilled as somehow less worthy of attention — whether from God or from others — then we are nothing. When love happens, we know it by its patience, kindness, and its ability to endure through all kinds of difficulties in order to confer its good. And happen it does! Who in your life helped you see the love of God? Who conferred this kind of love on you?

But the reality is that we cannot own this love with our own names or produce it through our own willpower. It can only come to us as a gift. On our own, we cannot produce the love that God has in mind: the kind that believes, hopes, and endures. Our sinfulness gets in the way! I'm not sure this is the conclusion that that Bible study wanted us to draw. I think that we were being encouraged to become better people, as though God would love us more if we could just become a little kinder, a little more humble. But if that is what Saint Paul wants us to do, then we are sunk! Because then all we will be doing is striving imperfectly and we will miss what is, in reality, God's gift.

The surprising truth is that, if you were going to ever substitute a name in for love in 1 Corinthians, it shouldn't be our names. There's only one name that you could really sub in for love there, and that is the name of Jesus. And all of the love we ever need comes from him and he will give it to us richly.

Jesus is patient. Actually, he has more patience than we could ever imagine. He suffers fools, hoping that they will come to him.

Jesus is kind.

He is not envious, arrogant, boastful, or rude.

He does not insist on his own way. He invites people to follow, coaxes them to join him at his table, live in his way. But he does not coerce or manipulate.

He is not irritable or resentful. He does not rejoice in wrong-doing, but even dies for wrong-doers, forgiving them from his cross. He rejoices in truth because he himself is the truth.

He bears all things, even our sins and our sorrows. Especially our sins and our sorrows.

He believes all things, even when we are short on faith. He's harder to offend than we are and so he endures all things. He hopes all things, even when we have given up.

When we can feel the love, the patience, the kindness, and the hope, when we see the world as Julian of Norwich must have seen it in her hazelnut, nothing to small or too large for love, when we live it, it is his spirit at work in us. When we cannot feel or see it or do it, his love is sufficient in itself.

And it never ends.

Amen.

Fifth Sunday after the Epiphany (SB)
1 Corinthians 15:1-11

Does Millard Fillmore Really Matter?

Now I would remind you, brothers and sisters, of the good news that I proclaimed to you, which you in turn received, in which also you stand, through which also you are being saved, if you hold firmly to the message that I proclaimed to you — unless you have come to believe in vain. For I handed on to you as of first importance what I in turn had received: that Christ died for our sins in accordance with the scriptures, and that he was buried, and that he was raised on the third day in accordance with the scriptures, and that he appeared to Cephas, then to the twelve. Then he appeared to more than five hundred brothers and sisters at one time, most of whom are still alive, though some have died. Then he appeared to James, then to all the apostles. Last of all, as to one untimely born, he appeared also to me. For I am the least of the apostles, unfit to be called an apostle, because I persecuted the church of God. But by the grace of God I am what I am, and his grace toward me has not been in vain. On the contrary, I worked harder than any of them — though it was not I, but the grace of God that is with me. Whether then it was I or they, so we proclaim and so you have come to believe.

We are now well in to the season of Epiphany. The word "epiphany" comes from a Greek word that in the most literal sense means "to shine on." Since we started this season with the story of the Wise Men (Magi) from the east traveling to see the infant Jesus by the light of a new star, the word is pretty spot on. In English, the word "epiphany" has a slightly broader meaning. An "epiphany" is a sudden insight. It is a revelation. The Bible stories we remember and contemplate during the season of Epiphany are all stories of how Jesus is revealed as the Messiah, the Son of God, and the true meaning of life. Epiphany is about how Jesus is shown to us; about how his light shines on us.

What all do you know about Jesus? You could make a pretty long list just of things that the Bible tells us about him. We know that he was born where animals were kept. We know that he did miraculous things and performed impossible healing. We know that he talked to the "wrong people" and listened to the wrong people and loved and valued the wrong people. We know he clashed with those in power and that they felt threated by him. We could list specific miracles, and rattle off quotes. We could make a roster of his followers; the twelve, and a good many more. We could draw up maps of his travels as people have done for ages. We don't know everything we'd like to. We have no idea what Jesus looked like, for example, or what he sounded like. We don't know a single thing he did from the age of twelve until he was "about thirty years old" (Luke 3:23). Yet even when you take into account all the gaps that scripture leaves unfilled, we still know a lot about Jesus.

What do we need to know about Jesus in order to be Christian? What do we need to believe about who Jesus is before we can consider ourselves to be disciples? It is enough simply to acknowledge that there was a rabbi in first century Palestine named Jesus of Nazareth? Surely that acknowledgment alone is not what it means to be Christian. Most atheists, and all serious historians, no matter how skeptical, admit that Jesus the person existed. Is it Christianity if you regard Jesus as a great teacher, and a positive moral example, like Siddhartha Gautama (the Buddha), or Mother Teresa, or Mr. Rogers? Do you have to be able to rattle off the names of the twelve apostles, or recite the Sermon on the Mount? Can you be wary of some of the miracle stories and be a Christian? In short, is being a Christian a matter of being a fan of Jesus, of being an admirer? On the other end, do you need to be a hard-core expert in all things New Testament to really follow Christ?

As we near the end of the season of Epiphany, we encounter a lesson from 1 Corinthians that goes some way toward answering that question.

Fifth Sunday after the Epiphany

For I handed on to you as of first importance what I in turn had received: that Christ died for our sins in accordance with the scriptures, and that he was buried, and that he was raised on the third day in accordance with the scriptures, and that he appeared to Cephas, then to the twelve.

The Bible tells us many things about Jesus, but here (and in a few other places) we are told what the basis of the Christian faith is. To know Jesus is to know the Son of God who died for our sin and who rose to give us life. To follow Jesus is to know that his very real death and his physical resurrection from the death matters to us, right now, two millennia later and half a world away; matters more than anything else has ever mattered and more than anything else ever will.

Being able to quote Jesus's parables doesn't make you a Christian. Knowing all the Jesus trivia in the world does not equal faith. Even holding Jesus up as the brightest guide to a good and moral life is not the same as being a disciple.

You may well know that Millard Fillmore (1800-1874) was the thirteenth president of the United States. You might have every confidence in the truth of that fact. You likely find no reason whatsoever to doubt it. But do you care? Does it really matter? Even if you are a direct descendent of President Fillmore, the fact of his presidency so long ago (1850-1853) has in all likelihood, absolutely zero impact on your day-to-day life.

Faith is not just the acknowledgment of fact. It's not simply admitting the reality of history. Faith is trust. Faith is dependence. Faith in Jesus is trust in, and dependence on, and attachment to Jesus. Faith changes your life. What is of first importance about Jesus Christ is how his presence in the world makes everything different forever. What is of first importance about Jesus Christ is that he died for you and rose for you and calls you to a bigger life now and into the future.

Jesus was a brilliant teacher and preacher, but of most importance, Jesus was God down to earth, God in the real world. God's love is revealed to us in the life of Jesus. To follow Jesus is to live for God and for others.

Down To Earth

Jesus walked on water and healed the sick; but of first importance, Jesus is where God meets us in our struggles, bearing our suffering. God's mercy is revealed to us in the death of Jesus. To follow Jesus is to bear his cross and be with those who are suffering.

Jesus upset the political and religious status quo of his age, but of first importance, he overturns death and sin and hopelessness in rising from the dead. God's glory is revealed to us in the resurrection of Jesus.

To follow Jesus is to proclaim hope and new life to all the world around us. This is of first importance.

Amen.

Sixth Sunday after the Epiphany (SB)
1 Corinthians 15:12-20

Elevator Speach

Now if Christ is proclaimed as raised from the dead, how can some of you say there is no resurrection of the dead? If there is no resurrection of the dead, then Christ has not been raised; and if Christ has not been raised, then our proclamation has been in vain and your faith has been in vain. We are even found to be misrepresenting God, because we testified of God that he raised Christ — whom he did not raise if it is true that the dead are not raised. For if the dead are not raised, then Christ has not been raised. If Christ has not been raised, your faith is futile and you are still in your sins. Then those also who have died in Christ have perished. If for this life only we have hoped in Christ, we are of all people most to be pitied.

But in fact Christ has been raised from the dead, the first fruits of those who have died.

They call it the 'elevator speech', or the 'elevator pitch'. Imagine that you've had a brilliant burst of creative genius; the 'aha' moment to end all 'aha' moments, your 'million-dollar idea'. This flash of insight could save countless lives, or could revolutionize life as we know it for the better, or could make you and lot of other people unreasonably rich, and make everyone's wallets just a bit thicker. We're just thinking here, so just go ahead and imagine that your idea could do all of those things. But here's the problem. For the time being, your idea is just an idea. It's a fantastic idea but it's stuck in the brain of someone (you) who doesn't have the experience and the know-how and the connections to make that idea into a reality.

Imagine that you are in an elevator going up to the eleventh floor. You are the only one in the elevator when it stops on three. In walks Elon Musk, Bill Gates, or whoever has all the experience and all the know-now and all the connections you could ever need. It is the opportunity of a lifetime. All you need is to convince this person that your idea is worth their attention. They push the button for the tenth floor, and the door closes. You have seven floors worth of elevator time, probably less than a minute, to summarize your life-altering, world-changing idea. Before the elevator stops on the tenth floor, and the doors open, the person who could make it all happen has to want to hear more. What do you say? How do you wrap up the biggest thing that's ever happened to the world into less than sixty seconds? Or how about we bring this example up to date. How do you change the world in a tweet? How do you summarize a mountain of thought into a one-liner? If you can't boil it all down to that one thing, that one sentence, then the rest doesn't really matter. No one will ever hear it.

The truth is that we do this all the time. We hear just a few words that stop us in our tracks and leave us needing to know more. "There's been an accident." "Firetrucks are headed to your house." "They've found a cure." "I'm pregnant." Those few words say everything, and yet there is so much more that you need to know. The whole idea of the elevator speech is to find that one, most important part of something much larger: that one thing that will convince people in an instant that they absolutely need to hear the rest.

Our second lesson for today includes Saint Paul's elevator speech. Not just Paul himself, but every Christian who has ever lived can get to the very heart of what their faith is truly all about with these few words: "But in fact, Christ has been raised from the dead." If that didn't happen, if Jesus didn't rise from the dead, then none of the rest of it really matters. If Jesus didn't rise from the dead, then he's a great teacher, a quick witted philosopher, a worker of miracles, but nothing more. If Jesus didn't rise from the dead, he's a prophet and a spokesman for the Word of God, but the world is full of those people. The Bible is full of those people. Yet we don't call Moses the Son of God. We don't wear little

Sixth Sunday after the Epiphany

hatchets around our necks to honor Elijah. Jesus is everything. Jesus is God in the flesh. Jesus is the one Moses and Elijah pointed to. Jesus is the Messiah and the Savior of the world. We know these things to be true, because Jesus rose from the dead.

"If Christ has not been raised" says Saint Paul, "your faith is futile", useless, impotent, meaningless "and you are still in your sins." "If Christ has not been raised" says Saint Paul, "Then those also who have died in Christ" are just going to have to stay dead. "If for this life only we have hoped in Christ", if for this life only we have given our lives in service; if for this life only we have let go of our greed and drive for self-promotion; if for this life only we have turned the other cheek and gone the extra mile and gladly put ourselves last, then we are the most pathetic people that there has ever been. If Jesus stayed dead, then our lives and our faith, have no life in them at all. The one thing that it all rides on is Jesus rising from the dead.

It really is the elevator speech. In the period of time after the resurrection, and before the gospels were written down (a span of three decades at the very least), if people knew one thing about Jesus, they knew that he had risen from the dead. None of the other stories about him would ever have been anything other than inspiring trivia, if Jesus had not, in the end, risen from the dead.

There is something in this elevator speech however, that makes it kind of a hard sell, and that is this. Jesus cannot possibly have risen from the dead. People don't do that. It just isn't possible. Saint Paul was fully aware of that. He wasn't naïve, or superstitious. Saint Paul wasn't gullible. He called the death and resurrection of Jesus "foolishness to Greeks" and a "stumbling block to the Jews". He knew it wasn't possible for Jesus to come back from the dead. At no point in history did anyone ever seriously believe that death could simply wear off. That happens in "Frankenstein", and in "E.T." It happens in myths, fairytales, and superhero movies. It doesn't happen in real life. But Jesus is part of history, and his death happened in real life and his rising happened in real life and that's just not possible. The Bible never says that the resurrection of Jesus is possible. The Bible only says

Down To Earth

that it happened. It may not be possible but it is real. It may not be logical, not even a little bit, but it is true.

If Christ has not been raised, your faith is futile and you are still in your sins. Then those also who have died in Christ have perished. If for this life only we have hoped in Christ, we are of all people most to be pitied. But in fact Christ has been raised from the dead, the first fruits of those who have died.

Jesus rose from the dead. If we lose sight of that, we're no longer looking at Jesus. Jesus rose from the dead is fact. It is history. It is reality. It is the truest thing that has ever happened. Jesus rose from the dead and it changed the world. It saved countless lives and revolutionized life as we know it for the better.

Amen.

Seventh Sunday after the Epiphany (KvD)
1 Corinthians 15:35-38; 42-50

Just A Box

But someone will ask, "How are the dead raised? With what kind of body do they come?" Fool! What you sow does not come to life unless it dies. And as for what you sow, you do not sow the body that is to be, but a bare seed, perhaps of wheat or of some other grain. But God gives it a body as he has chosen, and to each kind of seed its own body. So it is with the resurrection of the dead. What is sown is perishable, what is raised is imperishable. It is sown in dishonor, it is raised in glory. It is sown in weakness, it is raised in power. It is sown a physical body, it is raised a spiritual body. If there is a physical body, there is also a spiritual body. Thus it is written, "The first man, Adam, became a living being"; the last Adam became a life-giving spirit. But it is not the spiritual that is first, but the physical, and then the spiritual. The first man was from the earth, a man of dust; the second man is from heaven. As was the man of dust, so are those who are of the dust; and as is the man of heaven, so are those who are of heaven. Just as we have borne the image of the man of dust, we will also bear the image of the man of heaven. What I am saying, brothers and sisters, is this: flesh and blood cannot inherit the kingdom of God, nor does the perishable inherit the imperishable.

The funeral procession was about to begin. Behind the processional cross and the choir, the man's widow and sons stood. The oldest son was holding a small brass box with his father's ashes. As the organ swelled with the first notes of the hymn, the son's hands shook. He took deep breaths and repeated, over and over, "It's a box. It's just a box."

It was not just a box, of course, but the remains of the father who held him as an infant, hugged him as a child, and blessed him at his wedding. How is it that death reduces the people we

Down To Earth

love to ashes? How is it that a human being with an expansive imagination — who has traveled the world for example, or who read voraciously, or who planted large gardens and reaped their produce — now occupies but a small plot of cemetery ground? What do we make of this humiliation? It's no accident that funeral homes and cemetery employees prefer that we not witness the actual burial or committal of our loved ones. It's then when we see that after death, what is left over is dust.

The Christians in an ancient church in Corinth knew all about death's terrifying finality. When their pastor, Saint Paul, preached that they, like Jesus would be raised from dead with a physical body, they said, "No thanks." They had seen bodies become *things*, and they were content not to have that struggle anymore. It was better, they thought, to disregard the body entirely, to think of it as just a shell, just a box. I cannot blame the Corinthians for doubting the resurrection. After all, once it becomes clear what kinds of problems bodies cause, why would you ever want one back? What kind of body could ever allow us to avoid the agony of standing in a funeral procession with shaking hands, trying to convince ourselves, "it's just a box?" So, Saint Paul, how are the dead raised, and with what kind of body could they possibly come?

To help expand their imagination — and ours — Saint Paul draws on ancient science, which thought that seeds could only bring forth plants if they first fell into the earth and "died." We know now that seeds don't die; they germinate. But still, what comes forth from the seed — stem, leaves, flowers — is vastly different from the tiny brown grain that falls into the earth. Beyond the science of seeds (and in verses that are unfortunately omitted from this lectionary selection!), Saint Paul also reminds us that even in this world, there are different kinds of bodies and different kinds of flesh. A horse, a human, a flounder, and a hawk all have bodies, but not the same kind. The sun shines in one way and the moon in another. If we can recognize those orders of difference, Saint Paul thinks, then we are on our way toward understanding how the resurrection body could be something

Seventh Sunday after the Epiphany

other than the often problematic bodies we now have.

A woman in a congregation I once served looked forward to the resurrection with hope. A short, brown-haired woman, she always said jokingly that she hoped that in the resurrection of the dead, she would add a few inches to her height and perhaps trade out her unruly brown hair for golden curls. Her jokes always gave us a good laugh, and would inspire others to ask their own questions. In the resurrection, what age will we be? Will God take requests about our dimensions? Can we have the body of a 25-year-old but retain the wisdom and internal freedom we gain in later years?

Saint Paul did not answer these questions, and the scriptures contain no details about the precise details of our resurrection flesh. When Saint Paul tried to put substance on the idea of a resurrection body, he used words from the spiritual realm: "imperishable," "glory," "power," "spiritual," and "like the man from heaven." That last phrase is the clue to the meaning of all the other words. The man from heaven was Jesus, who was now imperishable, glorious, powerful, and spiritual. He also had a body, which Saint Paul had seen. As it went with Jesus, so it will go with us. Just as Jesus first lived among us as a physical being and now lives in the power of his resurrection, so it will happen to us. Now we live in our physical bodies, but some day — God's great getting-up day, some traditions call it — we too will live in that power.

As we ponder 1 Corinthians today, we are coming to the end of the season of Epiphany, and we are about to enter the great season of Lent. For many of us, Lent is an opportunity to reflect on the meaning of Jesus' own death and resurrection. Our church confesses, "he was crucified, died, and was buried." That last part is important. The scriptures allow us to witness what our funeral customs today often do not permit us to see. He was wrapped in linen cloths. He was laid in a new tomb. There were spices to camouflage the stench of decay. Someone rolled a stone before the cave to separate the living from the dead. Our creeds confess the finality: *he was buried*. No one expected that new life would

Down To Earth

burst forth from him like a seed germinating in the springtime.

Yet out from graveclothes and spices, beyond the stone, and within the tomb, God raised him up. *His body even in death was not a "thing."* His burial was the hinge between two orders of existence. In Epiphany, before we get to Lent, we have the opportunity to take in this reality. If we use Lent to meditate on Jesus' suffering and death as if he is only a unique example of God's resurrecting power and not also the template of our hope, then we will have missed the good news. From his life — which includes his death and requires his burial — comes more life.

Amen.

Transfiguration Sunday (SB)
2 Corinthians 3:12-4:2

Behind The Veil

Since, then, we have such a hope, we act with great boldness, not like Moses, who put a veil over his face to keep the people of Israel from gazing at the end of the glory that was being set aside. But their minds were hardened. Indeed, to this very day, when they hear the reading of the old covenant, that same veil is still there, since only in Christ is it set aside. Indeed, to this very day whenever Moses is read, a veil lies over their minds; but when one turns to the Lord, the veil is removed. Now the Lord is the Spirit, and where the Spirit of the Lord is, there is freedom. And all of us, with unveiled faces, seeing the glory of the Lord as though reflected in a mirror, are being transformed into the same image from one degree of glory to another; for this comes from the Lord, the Spirit.

Therefore, since it is by God's mercy that we are engaged in this ministry, we do not lose heart. We have renounced the shameful things that one hides; we refuse to practice cunning or to falsify God's word; but by the open statement of the truth we commend ourselves to the conscience of everyone in the sight of God.

Lent begins this week with Ash Wednesday, making today the last Sunday in the season of Epiphany. The word "Epiphany" comes from the Greek word that means "to shine on". The season of Epiphany began back in early January with the story of the wise men seeing a new star shining in the east and then using the star's position and its light to find the baby Jesus. The shining of that star showed people who Jesus is. Today the season comes to an end with a kind of bizarre bookend to the story that started it off. Today is Transfiguration Sunday, when we remember how Jesus himself shines with the glory of God. It's an odd story, to say the least, but it's easier to follow if you at least know who all the players are.

The story starts with Jesus and three of his closest followers up on a mountain top. It was also those three, Peter, James, and John, who went with Jesus to wake a recently deceased twelve-year-old girl back to life. It would be those three again who were with Jesus went he went off to pray in the garden of Gethsemane the night that Jesus was arrested. Peter, James, and John are the inner circle, or the 'executive committee' of the twelve disciples. Up on that mountain they see Jesus standing and shining like a spotlight revealing the glory of God, and flanked by Moses and Elijah.

Elijah was a prophet and a miracle worker early in the history of the kingdom of Israel. Elijah never died; instead he was taken up into heaven alive in a fiery chariot (2 Kings 2:11-12). It was widely believed that Elijah would return to announce the coming of God's chosen Messiah. Moses is the person whom God used to deliver the Hebrew people out of slavery in Egypt. Moses is the person to whom God gave the stone tablets of the Ten Commandments (twice!) Moses represents the law of God. Those are the characters in the story; Peter, James, John, Moses, and Elijah… and Jesus, of course. The whole story is about Jesus, of course. Peter, James and John are there because Jesus called them to follow him. Peter, James, and John were called to follow Jesus and to learn about Jesus. Where Jesus went, they followed, of course. They were there on that mountain, staring dumbfounded at the shining glory of Christ because Jesus wanted them to see, and eventually, to tell. Elijah and Moses were there. Elijah had been taken into heaven nearly a millennium before he stood on top of that mountain, pointing to Jesus with all the authority of the prophets. Moses, who had died just beyond the promised land many centuries before the time of Elijah, stood there in the halogen glow of Jesus's radiant glory with all the weight of history and all the might of the law of God. They were also there because of Jesus, of course. Elijah and Moses were there to reveal Jesus as the fulfillment of the words of the prophets, and as the

Transfiguration Sunday

ultimate goal of the freedom God gave through Moses.

Moses, oddly, had his own experience with luminescence. When Moses came down from Mount Sinai, carrying the stone slabs on which the Ten Commandments had been written, he was all aglow from his close encounter with God. You'd kind of expect this, but in the story (Exodus 34:29-35), Moses' glow was not metaphorical. Although he had no idea that this was happening at first, the skin of his face was literally putting off light. As you could imagine, this made normal social interaction a bit strained. It is safe to say that seeing such a thing would go well beyond distracting into terrifying. So in order to be able to interact with people, Moses covered his face with a veil, taking it off only when he was in the direct presence of God. This was his practice every day until the gleam of his face gradually faded away.

Until fairly recently, the idea of Moses veiling his face would be pretty difficult to relate to. It just wasn't something that you'd run into very often. Yes, there are certain religious traditions wherein people, women mostly, cover their faces out of modesty whenever they are in the presence of anyone other than immediate family. Something like that though is way outside of the experience of most Christians. Up until recently, the practice of covering your face in public was limited to operating rooms and bank robberies. Other than that, seeing someone out with their face covered in a cloth would have been considered peculiar at least, if not outright weird. Since the time of the coronavirus pandemic however, the sight of covered faces seems pretty ordinary to us. It is a sign of caution, but also a signal of compassion. Masks protect us from getting sick, and more importantly they keep us from making others sick. In spite of these benefits, we have all learned that there is a cost to covered faces. With masks on, you don't always recognize people you otherwise know, and they don't always recognize you. It's hard to understand what people are saying when they have a mask on, and it is hard to make yourself understood. Masks are barriers. Veils are barriers. That is their good side, and that is their downside. Masks isolate. Veils cut us off.

Down To Earth

After Moses and Elijah had gone, and as Jesus was headed back down off of the mountain with his "inner circle", he told Peter, James, and John not to tell anyone what they had seen "until after" Jesus had risen from the dead. The reason for this is pretty straightforward. On the mountain they had seen only part of the picture. On the mountain they had seen Jesus as the light of the world. On the mountain they had seen Jesus as the fulfillment and goal of the law and of the prophets. On the mountain they had heard the voice of God proclaiming Jesus to be God's beloved son. But they had not yet seen the horrible death of Jesus. They had not yet seen his world altering resurrection. Since they had not seen the cross, had not seen the empty tomb, they had not yet really seen Jesus. They hadn't yet seen all of it. The glory they had seen on the mountain was only part of it. So, until that time, until they had known Jesus as dead, until they saw the true brightness of the risen Christ, they had to keep quiet. For now, they had to keep a lid on things. For the time being, they had to cover up what they knew as if with a veil.

The time for veils is over now. God is keeping no secrets from us. The curtains have been pulled away and Jesus has been revealed. God's great truth has been unveiled for all the world. Because we can now plainly see the full glory of Jesus unmasked, we can now boldly say the whole truth of Jesus. Jesus is unveiled as the Son of God. Jesus is unveiled as the real meaning or scripture — the whole point of the law and the focus of the prophets' visions. Jesus is unveiled in his death for the redemption of the world. Jesus is unveiled by his empty grave. His burial shroud lay folded in the tomb, no longer covering anything. For us, there is no need of a veil. We don't have to keep quiet. The light of Christ shines in its fullness now. Speak Christ and be heard. Show Christ's love and be seen.

Amen.

Eighth Sunday after the Epiphany (SB)
1 Corinthians 15:51-58

The More Things Change

Listen, I will tell you a mystery! We will not all die, but we will all be changed, in a moment, in the twinkling of an eye, at the last trumpet. For the trumpet will sound, and the dead will be raised imperishable, and we will be changed. For this perishable body must put on imperishability, and this mortal body must put on immortality. When this perishable body puts on imperishability, and this mortal body puts on immortality, then the saying that is written will be fulfilled: "Death has been swallowed up in victory." "Where, O death, is your victory? Where, O death, is your sting?" The sting of death is sin, and the power of sin is the law. But thanks be to God, who gives us the victory through our Lord Jesus Christ.

Therefore, my beloved, be steadfast, immovable, always excelling in the work of the Lord, because you know that in the Lord your labor is not in vain.

In 1789, the year that the Constitution of the United States was ratified, founding father Benjamin Franklin wrote with his customary snarky wit: "Our new constitution is now established, and has an appearance that promised permanency; but in this world nothing can be said to be certain except death and taxes." Death and taxes do indeed seem to be among the few unwavering constants in the human experience. Nothing else ever seems to stay the same. Change is part of life and part of everything else, but that doesn't mean that we're okay with it.

Some things you always change — your socks for instance, or the oil in your car. Other things change and we adjust as a matter of course. Technology is constantly changing. Styles change. There are things that change even though we may not like it.

Down To Earth

Music comes into vogue and then goes out again, even if we would like our favorite genre to stick around forever. Businesses flourish and then vanish. Most adults can remember restaurant chains and nationwide stores, candy bars, and even brands of cars that just aren't there anymore. Roads and towns and ways of getting around change all the time. Even things that feel like they have always been the same and will never go away still change over time and sometimes disappear completely. Countries rise and countries fall. Languages change so thoroughly that people from different generations or different parts of the same country can have a hard time getting ideas across to each other.

Christians, particularly mainline Christians in liturgical denominations, have a reputation for being averse to change. Changes in worship, changes in church traditions, even a change in the color of the sanctuary carpet are all (according to the stereotype) met with great resistance.

"How many [insert your denomination here] does it take to change a light bulb?"

"Ten. One to change the bulb and nine to say they like the old bulb better."

"How many [insert your denomination here] does it take to change a light bulb?"

"Change? What do you mean change?"

"How many [insert your denomination here] does it take to change a light bulb?"

"They don't."

There is a supposedly true story of church treasurer who would go into the church building after the custodian had finished working, to remove any new light bulbs and put the burnt out ones back into place.

The real relationship of the Bible to change, or of Christianity to change is a bit more complicated than the stereotype. There are things that do not and cannot change. There is and will ever be only one God. God created the world and everything in it as the expression of love. God's promises never fail. God is Father, Son, and Holy Spirit. Jesus is the Son of God. Jesus is the Savior of the

Eight Sunday after the Epiphany

world. Christ has died. Christ is risen. Christ will come again. If you change any of those things, you are no longer talking about the true gospel. If you try to change any of those things, you have stepped outside of the realm of the Christian faith.

Beyond the unfaltering truth about the reality of God, and the powerful forgiveness and love of Jesus however, the message of the gospel is that *everything* changes.

"Listen, I will tell you a mystery! We will not all die, but we will all be changed, in a moment, in the twinkling of an eye, at the last trumpet. For the trumpet will sound, and the dead will be raised imperishable, and we will be changed." (1 Corinthians 15:51-52)

Humans are defined by their mortality. Death is part of life. Part of what makes us human is that our time is limited and our thoughts our limited, and our ability to do good is far tinier than we would like it to be. Humans are defined by their limits, but in Christ, all that changes.

"For the trumpet will sound, and the dead will be raised imperishable, and we will be changed." (1 Corinthians 15:51)

That change doesn't wait for the future. That change doesn't wait for the day of resurrection, and it certainly doesn't wait until we decide that we are ready. The world changed the day the risen Jesus stepped out of the darkness of his grave and walked true light into the world. You were changed the day you were baptized into the death and resurrection of our Lord. The story that upended reality became your story, and that story changed you. And every day, every second of every minute of every hour, you are made new as God's holy and perfect person, forgiven and loved and changed into the image of Christ.

In Christ, we are no longer defined by death. In Christ, we are no longer held in chains by our sin. In Christ, it is no longer our failures and our flaws that make us who we are. Jesus changes us. Jesus redeems us and forgives us and gives us life that not even death can stop. Jesus changes what it means to be human.

As clever as Benjamin Franklin was (and there's no denying his genius), and as funny as he was, it must be said that on close inspection, his quip about what is permanent ultimately misses the mark. Death may be certain, but it isn't permanent, it isn't final. Death indeed comes to all, but death has changed. Jesus has changed it. Death is no longer the end. In Christ, our perishable bodies have put on imperishability. Jesus has dressed our mortal bodies with immortality, and we have been changed. Death has been changed. The whole way the world works has been changed. The gospel of Jesus is the one thing that doesn't — and it has drastically and permanently changed absolutely everything else! At the risk of ruining Dr. Franklin's dark little joke, it too needs to be changed. How about this? "In this world nothing can be said to be certain except the love of Christ."

Amen.

Ninth Sunday after the Epiphany (KvD)
Galatians 1:1-12

Just One

Paul an apostle — sent neither by human commission nor from human authorities, but through Jesus Christ and God the Father, who raised him from the dead — and all the members of God's family who are with me, To the churches of Galatia: Grace to you and peace from God our Father and the Lord Jesus Christ, who gave himself for our sins to set us free from the present evil age, according to the will of our God and Father, to whom be the glory forever and ever. Amen.

I am astonished that you are so quickly deserting the one who called you in the grace of Christ and are turning to a different gospel — not that there is another gospel, but there are some who are confusing you and want to pervert the gospel of Christ. But even if we or an angel from heaven should proclaim to you a gospel contrary to what we proclaimed to you, let that one be accursed! As we have said before, so now I repeat, if anyone proclaims to you a gospel contrary to what you received, let that one be accursed!

Am I now seeking human approval, or God's approval? Or am I trying to please people? If I were still pleasing people, I would not be a servant of Christ. For I want you to know, brothers and sisters, that the gospel that was proclaimed by me is not of human origin; for I did not receive it from a human source, nor was I taught it, but I received it through a revelation of Jesus Christ.

The afterschool program at Galatia Lutheran Church was hitting its stride. Three years before, a team of energetic retired schoolteachers in the congregation noticed that an increasing number of children in the local elementary school came from homes where English was spoken as a second language and decided to put their church's building and their skills in service. Three days a week, children filled the Sunday school rooms with songs and crafts, ate their snacks, and received help with homework. Potential volunteers regularly called the church office asking how they could help. Checks came in the mail from people the church council had never heard of. Everything was great when two of the families showed up for Sunday morning worship. And everything was still great the Sunday after that. But a few months later, some of the kids sang a song in their families' original language during the time in the liturgy usually filled by the senior choir, and that's when things started going badly.

The newcomers to Galatia Lutheran Church were from a different culture than the original members of the congregation. The adults spoke with an accent, when they spoke English at all. The schoolteachers who had started the afterschool ministry were tickled pink to worship with their new students, but more than a few long-standing members were anxious. They'd never been sure about that afterschool program anyway. Weren't there other "ethnic" churches where these families could go, where they could be with their own people, where they might feel more comfortable? Phone calls were made. A petition was drawn up, asking the pastor to develop a relationship with another congregation where he could refer these new members. It only had a few signatures, but it caused a stir when it reached the church council. Everyone wondered how Pastor Scott would respond.

Pastor Scott could not sleep the week before the council meeting. He remembered the stories he had heard of how Galatia Lutheran Church had started. An Italian restaurant owner, a Catholic, had allowed a fledgling congregation to set up for Sunday worship in his banquet hall at low cost. In those days, relationships between Catholics and Lutherans on the matter of religion weren't all that easy, but somehow Giuseppe had made it work with the members of Galatia Lutheran Church.

Marianna, an old-timer who remembered those early days setting up the banquet hall chairs, had told him, "Well some

Ninth Sunday after the Epiphany

people didn't like it when we signed the contract, Pastor, but Giuseppe was so good to us. Can you imagine how all our complaints must have sounded to Jesus? There he is, suffering on the cross from our sins, and here we are standing at the foot of his cross complaining that the fellow downstairs is a Catholic. Doesn't the Bible say we're all one in Christ Jesus?"

"Aren't we all one in Christ Jesus?" thought Pastor Scott in his nighttime reverie. After all, the Bible does say that, in Galatians, no less. Maybe that's how Galatia Lutheran Church got its name. In the original Galatia, the ancient Galatia, there were both Jewish and Greek believers. In those days, Jews and Greeks didn't eat together or spend time in one another's homes. Jewish men were circumcised as they had been for thousands of years; Greeks were not. Greeks ate scallops and pork, Jews did not. The Galatian churches' first pastor, the apostle Paul, preached that Jesus had come to make one new humanity out of the two groups. His cross had broken down the dividing wall between them. The spirit of Christ was doing something brand new. This was the gospel: a new relationship with God and one another based on faith. But then a faction arose, telling them that they had gotten this one new humanity idea all wrong. The Greeks would have to become Jewish first, if they wanted to be a part of the church. The apostle Paul was astounded when he heard all that was going on in his little churches. Dividing people up was a human idea, it is not God's idea.

"Listen," the apostle Paul had preached, "neither circumcision nor uncircumcision is anything. A new creation is everything."

"Listen, as many of you who have been baptized into Christ have put on Christ, and there is no longer Jew nor Greek."

"Listen," the apostle Paul wrote to his congregation, "I'm astonished that you are so quickly deserting the one who called you in the grace of Christ and are turning to a different gospel — not that there is another gospel… But even if we or an angel from heaven should proclaim a gospel contrary to what we have proclaimed, let that one be accursed!"

Pastor Scott snuck out of bed and downstairs to write his

council report for that week's meeting. He suddenly felt inspired and knew exactly what he was going to say.

Listen, he said. Not everything that sounds good is good news. Not everything that's comfortable is the gospel. There's only one gospel: the one about Jesus, who calls us together into one new group. In the church, there are people who speak English and people who speak Vietnamese; people who speak Spanish and people who speak Urdu. We see that gospel when we come together as we've been doing since our afterschool ministry began. When we worship together, we show the world what heaven is like.

Listen, he said, Jesus alone saves us. The language we speak does not save us. The songs we sing do not save us. The food we eat at coffee hour does not save us. And more than anything else, feeling comfortable will not save us. For evidence of this, see the cross. Imagine yourself standing beneath Jesus' cross complaining that your neighbor's strange accent bothers you.

Listen, Galatia Lutheran Church, you once knew this gospel when you worshiped in an Italian Catholic's banquet hall. Then you got a taste of what God can make possible when people stay focused on Jesus. God revealed it to you as a gift!

Don't abandon that gospel now! Don't settle for human thoughts! Don't desert God's dream!

Amen.

www.ingramcontent.com/pod-product-compliance
Lightning Source LLC
Chambersburg PA
CBHW051713040426
42446CB00008B/859